THE AUSTRALIAN

Women's Weekly

back to basics

Toast
Grill
°C
60
90
120
150
180
210
240
POWER
On
Off
10
20
30
40
50
Min
60

Contents

The oven temperatures in this book are for conventional ovens; if you have a fan-forced oven, decrease the temperature by 10-20 degrees.

vegetables

cauliflower gratin

6 baby cauliflowers (750g), trimmed
45g (1½ ounces) butter
¼ cup (35g) plain (all-purpose) flour
1½ cups (375ml) hot milk
½ cup (60g) coarsely grated cheddar cheese
¼ cup (20g) finely grated parmesan cheese
1 tablespoon packaged breadcrumbs

1 Preheat oven to 220°C/425°F.
2 Boil, steam or microwave cauliflowers until tender; drain. Place in medium shallow ovenproof dish.
3 Meanwhile, melt butter in medium saucepan, add flour; cook, stirring, until mixture bubbles and thickens. Gradually stir in milk until smooth; cook, stirring, until mixture boils and thickens. Remove from heat, stir in cheeses.
4 Pour cheese sauce over cauliflower; sprinkle with breadcrumbs. Bake about 15 minutes or until browned lightly.

prep + cook time 30 minutes **serves** 6
nutritional count per serving 14.1g total fat (9g saturated fat); 865kJ (207 cal); 10.2g carbohydrate; 9.1g protein; 2.2g fibre

orange and maple glazed baby carrots

30g (1 ounce) butter
750g (1½ pounds) baby carrots, trimmed, peeled
2 teaspoons finely grated orange rind
¼ cup (60ml) orange juice
2 tablespoons dry white wine
2 tablespoons maple syrup
½ cup (70g) coarsely chopped roasted hazelnuts

1 Melt butter in large frying pan; cook carrots, turning occasionally, until almost tender.
2 Add rind, juice, wine and syrup to pan; bring to the boil. Reduce heat; simmer, uncovered, until liquid has almost evaporated and carrots are tender and caramelised.
3 Serve carrots sprinkled with nuts.

prep + cook time 25 minutes **serves** 4
nutritional count per serving 17.2g total fat (4.5g saturated fat); 1145kJ (274 cal); 20.8g carbohydrate; 4.1g protein; 7.7g fibre

perfect mashed potato

1kg (2 pounds) potatoes, chopped coarsely
45g (1½ ounces) butter
¾ cup (180ml) hot milk

1 Boil, steam or microwave potatoes until tender; drain.
2 Using the back of a wooden spoon; push potato through fine sieve into large bowl. Stir in butter and milk.

prep + cook time 30 minutes **serves** 4
nutritional count per serving 10.2g total fat (6.6g saturated fat); 1028kJ (246 cal); 30.1g carbohydrate; 6.7g protein; 3.4g fibre
tips Using hot milk instead of cold gives a creamier mash. Sebago, pink-eye or lasoda potatoes are all good choices.

sautéed potatoes

1kg potatoes, unpeeled
2 tablespoons olive oil
45g (1½ ounces) butter, chopped

1 Cut potatoes into 1cm slices.
2 Heat oil and butter in large frying pan; cook potato, covered, over medium heat, turning occasionally, until browned lightly. Reduce heat; cook, tossing pan to turn potato slices, about 10 minutes or until tender.

prep + cook time 25 minutes **serves** 4
nutritional count per serving 19.6g total fat (8g saturated fat); 1419kJ (339 cal); 32.8g carbohydrate; 6.1g protein; 4g fibre
note Desiree, bintje or russet burbank (idaho) potatoes are all good choices.

corn fritters

1 cup (150g) self-raising flour
½ teaspoon bicarbonate of soda (baking soda)
1 teaspoon ground cumin
¾ cup (180ml) milk
2 eggs, separated
2 cups (330g) fresh corn kernels
2 green onions (scallions), sliced thinly
2 tablespoons finely chopped fresh coriander (cilantro)

1 Sift flour, soda and cumin into medium bowl. Gradually whisk in milk and egg yolks until batter is smooth.
2 Beat egg whites in small bowl with electric mixer until soft peaks form.
3 Stir corn, onion and coriander into batter; fold in egg whites.
4 For each fritter, pour 2 tablespoons of the batter into heated oiled large frying pan; spread batter into round shape. Cook fritters about 2 minutes each side; remove from pan, cover to keep warm.
5 Repeat to make a total of 18 fritters.

prep + cook time 40 minutes **makes** 18
nutritional count per fritter 1.3g total fat (0.5g saturated fat); 263kJ (63 cal); 9.9g carbohydrate; 2.7g protein; 1.2g fibre

Serve with tomato chutney; sprinkle over fresh coriander leaves.

peas with mint butter

2¼ cups (350g) fresh shelled peas
45g (1½ ounces) butter, softened
1 tablespoon finely chopped fresh mint
1 teaspoon finely grated lemon rind

1 Boil, steam or microwave peas until tender; drain.
2 Meanwhile, combine remaining ingredients in small bowl.
3 Serve peas topped with butter mixture.

prep + cook time 10 minutes **serves** 4
nutritional count per serving 8.6g total fat (5.4g saturated fat); 589kJ (141 cal); 8.6g carbohydrate; 5.2g protein; 5g fibre
note You need approximately 1kg (2 pounds) fresh pea pods to get the required amount of shelled peas needed for this recipe.

asparagus hollandaise

1kg (2 pounds) asparagus, trimmed
HOLLANDAISE SAUCE
2 tablespoons water
2 tablespoons white wine vinegar
¼ teaspoon cracked black pepper
2 egg yolks
200g (6½ ounces) unsalted butter, melted

1 Make hollandaise sauce.
2 Boil, steam or microwave asparagus until tender. Serve asparagus on a large platter drizzled with hollandaise sauce.

HOLLANDAISE SAUCE Combine the water, vinegar and pepper in small saucepan; bring to the boil. Reduce heat; simmer, uncovered, until liquid is reduced to 1 tablespoon. Strain mixture through fine sieve into medium heatproof bowl; cool 10 minutes. Whisk egg yolks into vinegar mixture. Set bowl over medium saucepan of simmering water; do not allow water to touch base of bowl. Whisk mixture over heat until thickened. Remove bowl from heat; gradually whisk in melted butter in a thin, steady stream, whisking constantly until sauce is thick and creamy.

prep + cook time 35 minutes **serves** 4
nutritional count per serving 44g total fat (26.9g saturated fat); 1797kJ (430 cal); 2.8g carbohydrate; 6.1g protein; 2.6g fibre

hasselback potatoes

4 medium potatoes (800g), halved horizontally
45g (1½ ounces) butter, melted
2 tablespoons olive oil
¼ cup (25g) packaged breadcrumbs
½ cup (60g) finely grated cheddar cheese

1 Preheat oven to 180°C/350°F.
2 Place one potato half, cut-side down, on chopping board; place a chopstick on board along each side of potato. Slice potato thinly, cutting through to chopsticks to prevent cutting all the way through. Repeat with remaining potato halves.
3 Coat potatoes in combined butter and oil in medium baking dish; place, rounded-side up, in single layer. Roast 1 hour, brushing frequently with oil mixture.
4 Sprinkle combined breadcrumbs and cheese over potatoes; roast about 10 minutes or until golden brown.

prep + cook time 1 hour 30 minutes **serves** 4
nutritional count per serving 22.8g total fat (10g saturated fat); 1463kJ (350 cal); 24.5g carbohydrate; 8.8g protein; 3g fibre
note Desiree or ruby lou potatoes are good choices.

scalloped potatoes

1.2kg (2½ pounds) potatoes, peeled
155g (5 ounces) leg ham, chopped finely
1¼ cups (310ml) pouring cream (see notes)
¾ cup (180ml) milk
¾ cup (90g) coarsely grated cheddar cheese

1 Preheat oven to 180°C/350°F; oil 1.5-litre (6-cup) baking dish.
2 Using sharp knife, mandoline or V-slicer, slice potatoes into very thin slices; pat dry with absorbent paper. Layer a quarter of the potato in dish; top with a third of the ham. Continue layering remaining potato and ham, finishing with potato.
3 Heat cream and milk in small saucepan until almost boiling; pour over potato mixture. Cover with foil; bake in oven 30 minutes. Remove foil; bake 20 minutes. Top with cheese; bake, uncovered, about 20 minutes or until potato is tender. Stand 10 minutes before serving.

prep + cook time 1 hour 30 minutes **serves** 6
nutritional count per serving 29.5g total fat (18.8g saturated fat); 1864kJ (446 cal); 29.1g carbohydrate; 15.2g protein; 3.2g fibre
notes It is fine to use 1 x 300ml carton of cream for this recipe.
Desiree, coliban or sebago potatoes are all good choices.

prosciutto-wrapped bean bundles

200g (6½ ounces) green beans, trimmed
200g (6½ ounces) yellow beans, trimmed
8 slices prosciutto (90g)
60g (2 ounces) butter
1 tablespoon rinsed, drained baby capers
1 tablespoon lemon juice
⅓ cup coarsely chopped fresh flat-leaf parsley

1 Cook beans in medium saucepan of boiling water until just tender; drain. Rinse under cold water; drain. Divide beans into eight equal bundles.
2 Place prosciutto slices on board; top each with one bundle of beans. Wrap beans with prosciutto, rolling to enclose beans tightly.
3 Cook bean bundles in heated oiled large frying pan, turning, until prosciutto is crisp. Remove from pan; cover to keep warm.
4 Melt butter in same pan; cook capers, stirring, 1 minute. Stir in juice.
5 Serve bean bundles drizzled with caper mixture; sprinkle with parsley.

prep + cook time 30 minutes **serves** 8
nutritional count per serving 6.9g total fat (4.3g saturated fat); 347kJ (83 cal); 1.5g carbohydrate; 3.3g protein; 1.5g fibre

steamed asian greens with char siu sauce

1 fresh long red chilli, sliced thinly
345g (11 ounces) broccolini, trimmed
155g (5 ounces) snow peas, trimmed
2 baby buk choy (300g), halved
2 tablespoons char siu sauce
2 teaspoons sesame oil
1 tablespoon peanut oil
1 tablespoon toasted sesame seeds

1 Layer chilli, broccolini, snow peas and buk choy in large bamboo steamer lined with baking paper (parchment paper). Steam, covered, over large wok of simmering water about 5 minutes or until vegetables are just tender.
2 Combine vegetables, sauce and sesame oil in large bowl.
3 Heat peanut oil in small saucepan until hot; pour oil over vegetable mixture then toss to combine. Serve sprinkled with seeds.

prep + cook time 25 minutes **serves** 4
nutritional count per serving 9.5g total fat (1.4g saturated fat); 635kJ (152 cal); 7g carbohydrate; 6.6g protein; 6.6g fibre

creamed spinach

20g (¾ ounces) butter
625g (1¼ pounds) spinach, trimmed
½ cup (125ml) pouring cream

1 Melt butter in large frying pan; cook spinach, stirring, until wilted.
2 Add cream; bring to the boil. Reduce heat; simmer, uncovered, until liquid reduces by half.

prep + cook time 15 minutes **serves** 4
nutritional count per serving 38.7g total fat (25.4g saturated fat); 1555kJ (372 cal); 2.8g carbohydrate; 3.5g protein; 2.1g fibre

ratatouille

1 medium eggplant (300g), chopped coarsely
course cooking salt
1 medium red onion (170g)
2 tablespoons olive oil
1 clove garlic, crushed
1 small red capsicum (bell pepper) (150g), chopped coarsely
1 small green capsicum (bell pepper) (150g), chopped coarsely
2 medium zucchini (240g), sliced thickly
410g (13 ounces) canned crushed tomatoes
1 tablespoon tomato paste
1 tablespoon chopped fresh oregano

1 Place eggplant in colander, sprinkle with salt; stand 15 minutes. Rinse eggplant under cold water, drain well; pat dry with absorbent paper.
2 Cut onion into thin wedges. Heat half the oil in large frying pan, add onion, garlic and capsicums; cook, stirring, about 5 minutes or until onion is soft. Remove mixture from pan.
3 Heat remaining oil in same pan, add eggplant and zucchini; cook, stirring, about 5 minutes or until eggplant is browned lightly.
4 Return onion mixture to pan, add undrained tomatoes and paste; simmer, covered, about 20 minutes or until vegetables are tender. Stir in oregano.

prep + cook time 50 minutes (+ standing) **serves** 4
nutritional count per serving 9.9g total fat (1.3g saturated fat); 665kJ (159 cal); 11g carbohydrate; 4.1g protein; 5.5g fibre

salads

salade niçoise

200g (6½ ounces) baby green beans, trimmed
2 tablespoons olive oil
1 tablespoon lemon juice
2 tablespoons white wine vinegar
4 medium tomatoes (600g), cut into wedges
4 hard-boiled eggs, quartered
425g (13½ ounces) canned tuna in springwater, drained, flaked
½ cup (80g) rinsed, drained caperberries
½ cup (60g) seeded small black olives
¼ cup firmly packed fresh flat-leaf parsley leaves
440g (14 ounces) canned drained, whole baby new potatoes, rinsed, halved

1 Boil, steam or microwave beans until tender; drain. Rinse under cold water; drain.
2 Whisk oil, juice and vinegar in large bowl; add beans and remaining ingredients, mix gently.

prep + cook time 20 minutes **serves** 4
nutritional count per serving 16.9g total fat (3.7g saturated fat); 1522kJ (364 cal); 19.5g carbohydrate; 30.9g protein; 5.2g fibre

coleslaw

½ small cabbage (600g), shredded finely
1 medium carrot (120g), grated coarsely
4 green onions (scallions), sliced thinly
½ cup (150g) mayonnaise
1 tablespoon lemon juice

1 Combine ingredients in large bowl.

prep time 10 minutes **serves** 6
nutritional count per serving 8.1g total fat (1g saturated fat); 523kJ (125 cal); 8.8g carbohydrate; 2g protein; 4.5g fibre

potato salad

2kg (4 pounds) potatoes
2 tablespoons cider vinegar
4 green onions (scallions), sliced thinly
¼ cup finely chopped fresh flat-leaf parsley
MAYONNAISE
2 egg yolks
2 teaspoons lemon juice
1 teaspoon dijon mustard
1 cup (250ml) vegetable oil
2 tablespoons warm water, approximately

1 Cover peeled, whole potatoes with cold water in large saucepan; bring to the boil. Reduce heat; simmer, covered, until tender. Drain; cut into 3cm pieces. Spread potato on a tray, sprinkle with vinegar; refrigerate until cold.
2 Make mayonnaise.
3 Combine potato in large bowl with mayonnaise, onion and parsley.
MAYONNAISE Blend or process egg yolks, juice and mustard until smooth. With motor operating, gradually add oil in a thin, steady stream; process until mixture thickens. Add as much of the warm water as required to thin mayonnaise.

prep + cook time 45 minutes (+ refrigeration)
serves 8
nutritional count per serving 30.4g total fat (4.1g saturated fat); 1764kJ (422 cal); 29g carbohydrate; 6.2g protein; 3.7g fibre
note Sebago, bintje, desiree, kipfler and sebago potatoes are all good choices for this recipe.

tabbouleh

¼ cup (40g) burghul
3 medium tomatoes (450g)
3 cups coarsely chopped fresh flat-leaf parsley
3 green onions (scallions), chopped finely
¼ cup coarsely chopped fresh mint
¼ cup (60ml) lemon juice
¼ cup (60ml) olive oil

1 Place burghul in medium shallow bowl. Halve tomatoes, scoop pulp from tomato over burghul. Chop tomato flesh finely; spread over burghul. Cover; refrigerate 1 hour.
2 Combine burghul mixture in large bowl with remaining ingredients.

prep time 30 minutes (+ refrigeration) **serves** 4
nutritional count per serving 14.1g total fat (2g saturated fat); 790kJ (189 cal); 9.2g carbohydrate; 3.4g protein; 5.6g fibre

greek salad

¼ cup (60ml) olive oil
1 tablespoon lemon juice
1 tablespoon white wine vinegar
1 tablespoon finely chopped fresh oregano
1 clove garlic, crushed
3 medium tomatoes (450g), cut into wedges
2 lebanese cucumbers (260g), chopped coarsely
1 small red onion (100g), sliced thinly
1 small red capsicum (bell pepper) (150g), sliced thinly
½ cup (75g) seeded black olives
200g (6½ ounces) fetta cheese, chopped coarsely

1 Whisk oil, juice, vinegar, oregano and garlic in large bowl; add remaining ingredients, mix gently.

prep time 20 minutes **serves** 4
nutritional count per serving 25.8g total fat (9.6g saturated fat); 1359kJ (325 cal); 10.8g carbohydrate; 11.5g protein; 3.2g fibre

pasta salad

250g (8 ounces) orecchiette pasta
2 tablespoons drained sun-dried tomatoes in oil, chopped coarsely
1 small red onion (100g), sliced thinly
1 small green capsicum (bell pepper) (150g), sliced thinly
½ cup coarsely chopped fresh flat-leaf parsley

SUN-DRIED TOMATO DRESSING
1 tablespoon sun-dried tomato pesto
1 tablespoon white wine vinegar
2 tablespoons olive oil

1 Cook pasta in large saucepan of boiling water, uncovered, until just tender; drain. Rinse under cold water; drain.
2 Combine ingredients for sun-dried tomato dressing in screw-top jar; shake well.
3 Combine pasta in large bowl with remaining ingredients and dressing; toss gently.

prep + cook time 25 minutes **serves** 4
nutritional count per serving 12g total fat (1.9g saturated fat); 1405kJ (336 cal); 46g carbohydrate; 8.8g protein; 3.6g fibre

classic caesar

½ loaf ciabatta bread (220g)
1 clove garlic, crushed
⅓ cup (80ml) olive oil
2 eggs
3 baby cos lettuce, trimmed, leaves separated
1 cup (80g) flaked parmesan cheese

CAESAR DRESSING
1 clove garlic, crushed
1 tablespoon dijon mustard
2 tablespoons lemon juice
2 teaspoons worcestershire sauce
2 tablespoons olive oil

1 Preheat oven to 180°C/350°F.
2 To make croûtons, cut bread into 2cm (¾ inch) cubes; combine garlic and oil in large bowl with bread, place on oven tray. Toast bread, in oven, until croûtons are browned.
3 Combine ingredients for caesar dressing in screw-top jar; shake well.
4 Bring water to the boil in small saucepan, add eggs; cover pan tightly, remove from heat. Remove eggs from water after 2 minutes. When cool enough to handle, break eggs into large bowl (they will be runny), add lettuce; mix gently so egg coats leaves.
5 Add cheese, croûtons and dressing to bowl; toss gently.

prep + cook time 45 minutes **serves** 4
nutritional count per serving 39.1g total fat (9.1g saturated fat); 2366kJ (566 cal); 33.1g carbohydrate; 18.4g protein; 5.6g fibre

caprese salad

3 large egg (plum) tomatoes (270g), sliced thinly
310g (10 ounces) bocconcini cheese, drained, sliced thinly
2 tablespoons olive oil
¼ cup firmly packed fresh basil leaves, torn

1 Overlap slices of tomato and cheese on serving platter.
2 Drizzle with oil; sprinkle with basil.

prep time 15 minutes **serves** 4
nutritional count per serving 20.6g total fat (8.8g saturated fat); 1028kJ (246 cal); 1.6g carbohydrate; 13.6g protein; 1.1g fibre

oak leaf and mixed herb salad with dijon vinaigrette

1 green oak leaf lettuce, leaves separated
¼ cup coarsely chopped fresh chives
½ cup firmly packed fresh flat-leaf parsley leaves
½ cup firmly packed fresh chervil leaves
DIJON VINAIGRETTE
2 tablespoons olive oil
2 tablespoons white wine vinegar
1 tablespoon dijon mustard
2 teaspoons white sugar

1 Combine ingredients for dijon vinaigrette in screw-top jar; shake well.
2 Combine salad ingredients in medium bowl with dressing; toss gently.

prep time 10 minutes **serves** 6
nutritional count per serving 6.2g total fat (0.9g saturated fat); 288kJ (69 cal); 2g carbohydrate; 0.7g protein; 1.1g fibre

tuna salad

¼ cup (60ml) olive oil
2 tablespoons white wine vinegar
1 tablespoon lemon juice
2 teaspoons finely chopped fresh basil
2 teaspoons finely chopped fresh oregano
1 clove garlic, crushed
1 fresh long red chilli, chopped finely
1 medium iceberg lettuce, cut into wedges
425g (13½ ounces) canned tuna in springwater, drained, flaked
250g (8 ounces) cherry tomatoes, halved
1 medium avocado (250g), chopped coarsely
1 lebanese cucumber (130g), sliced thinly
1 small red onion (100g), sliced thinly

1 Combine oil, vinegar, juice, herbs, garlic and chilli in screw-top jar; shake well.
2 Place lettuce wedges on serving plate; top with remaining ingredients. Drizzle with dressing.

prep time 15 minutes **serves** 4
nutritional count per serving 26.1g total fat (4.9g saturated fat); 1492kJ (357 cal); 4.6g carbohydrate; 24.4g protein; 4.9g fibre

chicken salad

1 litre (4 cups) boiling water
1 litre (4 cups) chicken stock
750g (1½ pounds) chicken breast fillets
1 long french bread stick, sliced thinly
2 tablespoons olive oil
½ cup (150g) mayonnaise
½ cup (120g) sour cream
2 tablespoons lemon juice
4 stalks celery (600g), trimmed, sliced thinly
1 medium white onion (150g), chopped finely
3 large dill pickles (150g), sliced thinly
2 tablespoons finely chopped fresh flat-leaf parsley
1 tablespoon finely chopped fresh tarragon
1 large butter (boston) lettuce, leaves separated

1 Bring the water and stock to the boil in large saucepan, add chicken; simmer, covered, about 10 minutes or until chicken is cooked through. Cool chicken in liquid 10 minutes; slice thinly. Discard liquid.
2 Meanwhile, brush both sides of bread slices with oil; toast under preheated grill (broiler) until browned lightly both sides.
3 Whisk mayonnaise, sour cream and juice in small bowl. Combine chicken with celery, onion, pickle and herbs in large bowl; toss gently.
4 Place lettuce leaves on serving platter; top with salad and bread, drizzle with mayonnaise mixture.

prep + cook time 55 minutes **serves** 4
nutritional count per serving 47.3g total fat (14.6g saturated fat); 3566kJ (853 cal); 52.1g carbohydrate; 52.2g protein; 6.3g fibre

classic mayonnaise

2 egg yolks
½ teaspoon salt
1 teaspoon dijon mustard
⅔ cup (160ml) extra light olive oil
⅓ cup (80ml) olive oil
1 tablespoon white wine vinegar
1 tablespoon lemon juice

1 Combine egg yolks, salt and mustard in medium bowl. Gradually add oils in a thin, steady stream, whisking constantly until mixture thickens. Stir in vinegar and juice.

prep time 15 minutes **makes** 1 cup
nutritional count per tablespoon 19.2g total fat (2.9g saturated fat); 719kJ (172 cal); 0g carbohydrate; 0.5g protein; 0g fibre

french dressing

⅓ cup (80ml) white wine vinegar
2 teaspoons dijon mustard
1 teaspoon caster sugar
⅔ cup (160ml) olive oil

1 Whisk vinegar, mustard and sugar in small jug until smooth; gradually whisk in oil, in a thin steady stream, until thickened.

prep time 5 minutes **makes** 1 cup
nutritional count per tablespoon 12.1g total fat (1.7g saturated fat); 456kJ (109 cal); 0.4g carbohydrate; 0g protein; 0g fibre

curries

butter chicken

1 cup (150g) unsalted raw cashews
2 teaspoons garam masala
2 teaspoons ground coriander
½ teaspoon chilli powder
3 cloves garlic, chopped coarsely
4cm (1½ inch) piece fresh ginger (20g), grated
2 tablespoons white vinegar
⅓ cup (95g) tomato paste
½ cup (140g) yogurt
1kg (2 pounds) chicken thigh fillets, halved
75g (2½ ounces) butter
1 large brown onion (200g), chopped finely
1 cinnamon stick
4 cardamom pods, bruised
1 teaspoon hot paprika
410g (13 ounces) canned tomato puree
¾ cup (180ml) chicken stock
¾ cup (180ml) pouring cream

1 Dry-fry nuts, garam masala, coriander and chilli in small frying pan, stirring, until nuts are browned lightly.
2 Blend or process nut mixture with garlic, ginger, vinegar, paste and half the yogurt until mixture forms a paste. Transfer to large bowl, stir in remaining yogurt and chicken. Cover; refrigerate 3 hours or overnight.
3 Melt butter in large saucepan; cook onion, cinnamon and cardamom, stirring, until onion is browned lightly. Add chicken mixture; cook, stirring, 10 minutes.
4 Stir in paprika, puree and stock; simmer, uncovered, 45 minutes, stirring occasionally.
5 Discard cinnamon and cardamom. Add cream; simmer, uncovered, 5 minutes.

prep + cook time 1 hour 40 minutes (+ refrigeration)
serves 4
nutritional count per serving 74g total fat (33.3g saturated fat); 4138kJ (990 cal); 20.8g carbohydrate; 59.3g protein; 6.5g fibre

panang fish curry

820ml (26 ounces) canned coconut milk
¼ cup (60g) bottled panang curry paste (see notes)
¼ cup (60ml) fish sauce
2 tablespoons grated palm sugar
4 fresh kaffir lime leaves, torn
2 tablespoons peanut oil
500g (1 pound) ling fillets (see notes), cut into 3cm pieces
500g (1 pound) uncooked medium king prawns (shrimp)
250g (8 ounces) scallops
200g (6½ ounces) snake beans, chopped coarsely
½ cup loosely packed fresh thai basil leaves
½ cup (70g) chopped roasted unsalted peanuts
2 fresh long red chillies, sliced thinly

1 Place coconut milk, paste, sauce, sugar and lime leaves in wok; simmer, stirring, about 15 minutes or until mixture reduces by about a third.
2 Meanwhile, heat oil in large frying pan; cook seafood, in batches, until just changed in colour. Drain on absorbent paper.
3 Add beans and seafood to curry mixture; cook, uncovered, stirring occasionally, about 5 minutes or until beans are just tender and seafood is cooked as desired.
4 Serve curry sprinkled with basil, nuts and chilli.

prep + cook time 45 minutes **serves** 4
nutritional count per serving 64.3g total fat (39.8g saturated fat); 3716kJ (889 cal); 18.3g carbohydrate; 57.1g protein; 7.2g fibre
notes If you want to make your own curry paste, use the recipe below.
You can use any firm white fish fillets you like.

panang curry paste

25 dried long red chillies
1 teaspoon ground coriander
2 teaspoons ground cumin
2 cloves garlic, quartered
8 green onions (scallions), chopped coarsely
2 x 10cm (4 inch) sticks fresh lemon grass (40g), sliced thinly
2cm (¾ inch) piece fresh galangal (10g), chopped finely
2 teaspoons shrimp paste
½ cup (75g) roasted unsalted peanuts
2 tablespoons peanut oil

1 Place chillies in small heatproof jug, cover with boiling water; stand 15 minutes, drain.
2 Meanwhile, dry-fry coriander and cumin in small frying pan over medium heat, stirring until fragrant.
3 Blend or process chillies and spices with remaining ingredients until mixture forms a paste.

prep + cook time 25 minutes (+ standing)
makes 1 cup
nutritional count per tablespoon 6.1g total fat (0.9g saturated fat); 288kJ (69 cal); 1.3g carbohydrate; 1.9g protein; 0.9g fibre

easy lamb curry

2 cloves garlic, crushed
2 long green chillies, chopped
5cm (2 inch) piece fresh ginger (25g), peeled, chopped
2 tablespoons vegetable oil
2 medium brown onions (300g), chopped coarsely
1½ teaspoons ground turmeric
1 teaspoon ground cumin
3 teaspoons ground coriander
1 teaspoon ground chilli powder
1kg (2 pounds) diced lamb shoulder
1 teaspoon salt
410g (13 ounces) canned diced tomatoes
¼ cup (60ml) coconut cream

1 Using mortar and pestle (or small processor), pound garlic, chilli and ginger to form a paste.
2 Heat oil in large saucepan; cook onion, stirring, about 10 minutes or until browned lightly. Add garlic paste; cook, stirring, over low heat, 3 minutes or until fragrant but not browned.
3 Blend spices with a little water to make a smooth paste, add to pan; cook, stirring, 5 minutes.
4 Cook lamb, in batches, in pan with spice mix until browned. Return lamb to pan with salt. Add undrained tomatoes; mix well.
5 Cook curry, covered, stirring occasionally, about 50 minutes or until lamb is tender. Stir in coconut cream in the last 20 minutes of cooking time.

prep + cook time 1 hour 30 minutes **serves** 4
nutritional count per serving 26.9g total fat (10.6g saturated fat); 2052kJ (491 cal); 8.4g carbohydrate; 52.4g protein; 3g fibre

green chicken curry

1 tablespoon peanut oil
¼ cup (75g) bottled green curry paste (see note)
3 long green chillies, chopped finely
1kg (2 pounds) chicken thigh fillets, cut into 3cm pieces
820ml (26 ounces) canned coconut milk
2 tablespoons fish sauce
2 tablespoons lime juice
1 tablespoon grated palm sugar
155g (5 ounces) pea eggplants
1 large zucchini (150g), sliced thinly
⅓ cup loosely packed fresh thai basil leaves
¼ cup loosely packed fresh coriander (cilantro) leaves
2 green onions (scallions), chopped coarsely

1 Heat oil in large saucepan; cook paste and about two-thirds of the chilli, stirring, about 2 minutes or until fragrant. Add chicken; cook, stirring, until browned.
2 Add coconut milk, sauce, juice, sugar and eggplants; simmer, uncovered, about 10 minutes or until eggplants are just tender.
3 Add zucchini, basil and coriander; simmer, uncovered, until zucchini is just tender.
4 Serve curry sprinkled with remaining chilli and green onion.

prep + cook time 45 minutes **serves** 4
nutritional count per serving 67.3g total fat (43.2g saturated fat); 3716kJ (889 cal); 17g carbohydrate; 52.9g protein; 6g fibre
note If you want to make your own curry paste, use the recipe below.

green curry paste

2 teaspoons ground coriander
2 teaspoons ground cumin
10 long green chillies, chopped coarsely
10 small green chillies, chopped coarsely
1 teaspoon shrimp paste
1 clove garlic, quartered
4 green onions (scallions), chopped coarsely
10cm (4 inch) stick fresh lemon grass (20g), chopped finely
1cm (½ inch) piece fresh galangal (5g), chopped finely
¼ cup coarsely chopped fresh coriander (cilantro) root and stem mixture
1 tablespoon peanut oil

1 Dry-fry ground coriander and cumin in small frying pan over medium heat, stirring until fragrant.
2 Blend or process spices with chillies, paste, garlic, onion, lemon grass, galangal and coriander mixture until mixture forms a paste.
3 Add oil to paste; continue to blend until smooth.

prep + cook time 25 minutes **makes** 1 cup
nutritional count per tablespoon 1.6g total fat (0.3g saturated fat); 67kJ (16 cal); 0.3g carbohydrate; 0.2g protein; 0.2g fibre
note When purchasing coriander, make sure you buy stems that also have the root attached for this recipe. Wash well before using.

beef massaman curry

1kg (2 pounds) beef skirt steak, cut into 3cm pieces
2 cups (500ml) beef stock
5 cardamom pods, bruised
¼ teaspoon ground clove
2 star anise
1 tablespoon grated palm sugar
2 tablespoons fish sauce
2 tablespoons tamarind concentrate
820ml (26 ounces) canned coconut milk
2 tablespoons bottled massaman curry paste (see note)
8 baby brown onions (200g), halved
1 medium kumara (orange sweet potato) (400g), chopped coarsely
¼ cup (35g) chopped roasted unsalted peanuts
2 green onions (scallions), sliced thinly

1 Place beef, 1½ cups of the stock, cardamom, clove, star anise, sugar, sauce, 1 tablespoon of the tamarind and half the coconut milk in large saucepan; simmer, uncovered, about 1½ hours or until beef is almost tender.
2 Strain beef over large bowl; reserve 1 cup braising liquid, discard remainder. Cover beef to keep warm.
3 Cook curry paste in same pan, stirring, until fragrant. Add remaining coconut milk, tamarind and stock; bring to the boil. Cook, stirring, about 1 minute or until mixture is smooth. Return beef to pan with brown onion, kumara and reserved braising liquid; simmer, uncovered, about 30 minutes or until beef and vegetables are tender.
4 Stir nuts and green onion into curry off the heat.

prep + cook time 2 hours 30 minutes **serves** 4
nutritional count per serving 52.7g total fat (39.5g saturated fat); 3645kJ (872 cal); 29.2g carbohydrate; 67.4g protein; 7.2g fibre
note If you want to make your own curry paste, use the recipe below.

massaman curry paste

20 dried long red chillies
1 teaspoon ground coriander
2 teaspoons ground cumin
2 teaspoons ground cinnamon
½ teaspoon ground cardamom
½ teaspoon ground clove
5 cloves garlic, quartered
1 large brown onion (200g), chopped coarsely
2 x 10cm (2 inch) sticks fresh lemon grass (40g), thinly sliced
3 fresh kaffir lime leaves, sliced thinly
4cm (1½ inch) piece fresh ginger (20g), chopped coarsely
2 teaspoons shrimp paste
1 tablespoon peanut oil

1 Preheat oven to 180°C/350°F.
2 Place chillies in small heatproof jug, cover with boiling water; stand 15 minutes, drain.
3 Meanwhile, dry-fry coriander, cumin, cinnamon, cardamom and clove in small frying pan, stirring until fragrant.
4 Place chillies and spices in small shallow baking dish with remaining ingredients. Roast, uncovered, 15 minutes.
5 Blend or process roasted curry paste mixture, or crush using mortar and pestle, until smooth.

prep + cook time 35 minutes (+ standing)
makes 1 cup
nutritional count per tablespoon 1.7g total fat (0.3g saturated fat); 105kJ (25 cal); 1.5g carbohydrate; 0.5g protein; 0.4g fibre

potato and pea curry

3 medium potatoes (600g), chopped coarsely
1 tablespoon vegetable oil
2 cloves garlic, crushed
2cm (¾ inch) piece fresh ginger (10g), grated
¼ cup (75g) tikka masala curry paste
1¼ cups (310ml) pouring cream (see note)
1½ cups (180g) frozen peas
½ cup (140g) yogurt
2 tablespoons lime juice
4 small pappadams
4 hard-boiled eggs, halved

1 Boil, steam or microwave potato until just tender; drain.
2 Meanwhile, heat oil in large saucepan; cook garlic and ginger, stirring, 2 minutes. Add paste; cook, stirring, until fragrant.
3 Add cream, bring to the boil; reduce heat. Add potato; simmer, uncovered, 5 minutes. Add peas and yogurt; stir over low heat about 5 minutes or until peas are heated through. Stir in juice.
4 Cook pappadams, in microwave oven, following packet instructions.
5 Top curry with egg; serve with pappadams.

prep + cook time 40 minutes **serves** 4
nutritional count per serving 51.8g total fat (25.5g saturated fat); 3106kJ (743 cal); 37.8g carbohydrate; 22.7g protein; 24.5g fibre
note It is fine to use 1 x 300ml carton of cream for this recipe.

beef rendang

1.5kg (3 pounds) beef chuck steak, trimmed, cut into 3cm cubes
410ml (13 ounces) canned coconut milk
½ cup (125ml) water
10cm (4 inch) stick fresh lemon grass (20g), bruised
3 fresh kaffir lime leaves, torn

SPICE PASTE
2 medium red onions (340g), chopped coarsely
4 cloves garlic, chopped coarsely
5cm (2 inch) piece fresh ginger (25g), chopped coarsely
2 fresh long red chillies, chopped coarsely
3 teaspoons grated fresh galangal
3 teaspoons ground coriander
1½ teaspoons ground cumin
1 teaspoon ground turmeric
1 teaspoon salt

1 Blend or process spice paste ingredients until combined.

2 Combine paste in wok with beef, coconut milk, the water, lemon grass and lime leaves; bring to the boil. Reduce heat; simmer, covered, stirring occasionally, about 2 hours or until mixture thickens and beef is tender.

prep + cook time 2 hours 15 minutes **serves** 6
nutritional count per serving 25.2g total fat (16.9g saturated fat); 1952kJ (467 cal); 6.1g carbohydrate; 52.9g protein; 2.5g fibre

Serve with steamed jasmine rice and combined finely chopped cucumber and finely sliced fresh red chilli in rice vinegar.

red beef curry

1 tablespoon peanut oil
4 beef scotch fillet steaks (500g)
¼ cup (75g) bottled red curry paste (see note)
220g (7 ounces) canned bamboo shoots, drained, rinsed
820ml (26 ounces) canned coconut cream
½ cup (125ml) beef stock
2 tablespoons fish sauce
2 tablespoons lime juice
2 fresh kaffir lime leaves, shredded finely
4 large zucchini (600g), sliced thinly
⅓ cup firmly packed fresh thai basil leaves

1 Heat oil in large flameproof casserole dish; cook beef, in batches, until browned. Remove from dish.
2 Cook paste in same dish, stirring, until fragrant. Return beef to dish with bamboo shoots, coconut cream, stock, sauce, juice and lime leaves; simmer, uncovered, 1 hour 20 minutes. Add zucchini, simmer about 5 minutes or until tender.
3 Serve curry sprinkled with basil.

prep + cook time 1 hour 50 minutes **serves** 4
nutritional count per serving 55.5g total fat (40.6g saturated fat); 2897kJ (693 cal); 12.3g carbohydrate; 34.1g protein; 7.2g fibre
note If you want to make your own curry paste, use the recipe below.

red curry paste

20 dried long red chillies
1 teaspoon ground coriander
2 teaspoons ground cumin
1 teaspoon hot paprika
2cm (¾ inch) piece fresh ginger (10g), chopped coarsely
3 cloves garlic, quartered
1 medium red onion (170g), chopped coarsely
2 x 10cm (4 inch) sticks fresh lemon grass (40g), sliced thinly
2 tablespoons coarsely chopped fresh coriander (cilantro) root and stem mixture
2 teaspoons shrimp paste
1 tablespoon peanut oil

1 Place chillies in small heatproof jug, cover with boiling water; stand 15 minutes, drain.
2 Meanwhile, dry-fry ground coriander, cumin and paprika in small frying pan, stirring until fragrant.
3 Blend or process chillies and spices with ginger, garlic, onion, lemon grass, coriander mixture and paste until mixture forms a paste.
4 Add oil to paste; continue to blend until smooth.

prep + cook time 25 minutes (+ standing)
makes 1 cup
nutritional count per tablespoon 1.6g total fat (0.3g saturated fat); 92kJ (22 cal); 1.2g carbohydrate; 0.4g protein; 0.5g fibre

stews

chilli con carne

- 1 cup (200g) dried kidney beans
- 1.5kg (3 pounds) beef chuck steak
- 2 litres (8 cups) water
- 1 tablespoon olive oil
- 2 medium brown onions (300g), chopped coarsely
- 2 cloves garlic, crushed
- 2 teaspoons ground cumin
- 2 teaspoons ground coriander
- ½ teaspoon cayenne pepper
- 2 teaspoons sweet paprika
- 820g (26 ounces) canned crushed tomatoes
- 1 tablespoon tomato paste
- 4 green onions (scallions), chopped coarsely
- 2 tablespoons coarsely chopped fresh coriander (cilantro)
- ⅓ cup (65g) finely chopped bottled jalapeño chillies

1 Place beans in medium bowl, cover with water; stand overnight, drain.

2 Combine beef with the water in large saucepan; bring to the boil. Reduce heat, simmer, covered, 1½ hours.

3 Drain beef in large muslin-lined strainer over bowl; reserve 3½ cups of the cooking liquid. Using two forks, shred beef.

4 Heat oil in same pan; cook brown onion and garlic, stirring, until onion is soft. Add spices; cook, stirring, until fragrant. Add beans, undrained tomatoes, paste and 2 cups of the reserved liquid; bring to the boil, then simmer, covered, 1 hour.

5 Add beef and remaining reserved liquid to pan; simmer, covered, about 30 minutes or until beans are tender. Remove from heat; stir in green onions, fresh coriander and chilli.

prep + cook time 3 hours 45 minutes (+ standing)
serves 8
nutritional count per serving 11.4g total fat (3.9g saturated fat); 1496kJ (358 cal); 14.7g carbohydrate; 45.1g protein; 7.6g fibre

Serve with steamed rice and warm flour tortillas.

coq au vin

750g (1½ pounds) spring onions
¼ cup (60ml) olive oil
6 rindless bacon slices (390g), chopped coarsely
280g (9 ounces) button mushrooms
2 cloves garlic, crushed
8 chicken thigh fillets (880g)
¼ cup (35g) plain (all-purpose) flour
2 cups (500ml) dry red wine
1½ cups (375ml) chicken stock
2 tablespoons tomato paste
3 bay leaves
4 sprigs fresh thyme
2 sprigs fresh rosemary

1 Trim green ends from onions, leaving about 4cm of stem attached; trim roots. Heat 1 tablespoon of the oil in large frying pan; cook onions, stirring, until browned all over; remove from pan.
2 Add bacon, mushrooms and garlic to pan; cook, stirring, until bacon is crisp, remove from pan.
3 Coat chicken in flour; shake off excess. Heat remaining oil in same pan. Cook chicken, in batches, until browned all over; drain on absorbent paper.
4 Return chicken to pan with wine, stock, paste, bay leaves, herbs, onions and bacon mixture. Bring to the boil; reduce heat, simmer, uncovered, about 35 minutes or until chicken is tender and sauce has thickened slightly.

prep + cook time 1 hour 30 minutes **serves** 4
nutritional count per serving 43.6g total fat (11.8g saturated fat); 3428kJ (820 cal); 16.3g carbohydrate; 67.8g protein; 6.4g fibre

osso buco

6 pieces veal osso buco (1.8kg)
½ cup (75g) plain (all-purpose) flour
45g (1½ ounces) butter
2 tablespoons olive oil
3 stalks celery (450g), trimmed, chopped coarsely
6 drained anchovy fillets, chopped coarsely
¾ cup (180ml) dry white wine
820g (26 ounces) canned diced tomatoes
½ cup (125ml) chicken stock
5 cloves garlic, crushed
3 bay leaves
10 fresh thyme sprigs

GREMOLATA
½ cup finely chopped fresh flat-leaf parsley
2 cloves garlic, chopped finely
1 teaspoon finely grated lemon rind

1 Preheat oven to 160°C/325°F.
2 Coat veal in flour; shake off excess. Heat butter and oil in large frying pan; cook veal, in batches, until browned both sides. Transfer veal to large ovenproof dish.
3 Cook celery and anchovy in same pan, stirring, until celery softens. Add wine; bring to the boil. Stir in undrained tomatoes, stock, garlic, bay leaves and thyme; return to the boil.
4 Pour tomato mixture over veal. Cook, covered, in oven about 1½ hours or until veal starts to fall from the bone.
5 Meanwhile, make gremolata.
6 Serve osso buco sprinkled with gremolata.
gremolata Combine ingredients in small bowl.

prep + cook time 2 hours **serves** 6
nutritional count per serving 13.2g total fat (4.8g saturated fat); 1626kJ (389 cal); 14.4g carbohydrate; 46.1g protein; 3.8g fibre
note Standing the veal pieces upright in the pan, rather than laying them down, helps to keep the delicious bone marrow intact.

Serve with soft polenta.

lamb, apricot and almond tagine

2 tablespoons olive oil
1kg (2 pounds) diced lamb
2 cloves garlic, crushed
2cm (¾ inch) piece fresh ginger (10g), grated
12 shallots (300g), halved
1 medium red capsicum (bell pepper) (200g), chopped coarsely
1 teaspoon ground cumin
1½ cups (375ml) water
1½ cups (375ml) chicken stock
½ teaspoon saffron threads
1 cup (150g) dried apricots halves
1 tablespoon finely chopped preserved lemon rind
200g (6½ ounces) green beans, trimmed, chopped coarsely
½ cup (70g) slivered almonds

1 Heat half the oil in large saucepan; cook lamb, in batches, until browned. Remove from pan.
2 Heat remaining oil in same pan; cook garlic, ginger, shallot, capsicum and cumin, stirring, until fragrant.
3 Return lamb to pan; add the water, stock and saffron, bring to the boil. Reduce heat; simmer, covered, about 1 hour or until lamb is tender. Add apricots, lemon and beans; simmer, uncovered, 15 minutes.
4 Serve tagine sprinkled with nuts.

prep + cook time 1 hour 50 minutes **serves** 4
nutritional count per serving 41.7g total fat (12.1g saturated fat); 3018kJ (722 cal); 22.1g carbohydrate; 61.3g protein; 7.8g fibre
note Preserved lemon is a North African specialty; lemons are quartered and preserved in salt and lemon juice or water. To use, remove and discard pulp, squeeze juice from rind, rinse rind well; slice thinly. They are available from Middle-Eastern food stores and many larger supermarkets.

boeuf bourguignon

280g (9 ounces) baby brown onions
2 tablespoons olive oil
2kg (4 pounds) gravy beef, trimmed, chopped coarsely
30g (1 ounce) butter
4 rindless bacon slices (260g), chopped coarsely
410g (13 ounces) button mushrooms, halved
2 cloves garlic, crushed
¼ cup (35g) plain (all-purpose) flour
1¼ cups (310ml) beef stock
2½ cups (625ml) dry red wine
2 bay leaves
2 sprigs fresh thyme
½ cup coarsely chopped fresh flat-leaf parsley

1 Peel onions, leaving root end intact so onion remains whole during cooking.
2 Heat oil in large flameproof dish; cook beef, in batches, until browned. Remove from pan.
3 Add butter to dish; cook onions, bacon, mushrooms and garlic, stirring, until onions are browned lightly.
4 Sprinkle flour over onion mixture; cook, stirring, until flour mixture thickens and bubbles. Gradually add stock and wine; stir over heat until mixture boils and thickens. Return beef and any juices to dish, add bay leaves and thyme; bring to the boil. Reduce heat; simmer, covered, about 2 hours or until beef is tender, stirring every 30 minutes.
5 Remove from heat; discard bay leaves. Stir in parsley.

prep + cook time 2 hours 45 minutes **serves** 6
nutritional count per serving 31.4g total fat (12.1g saturated fat); 2658kJ (636 cal); 6.6g carbohydrate; 80.3g protein; 2.8g fibre

Serve with garlic mashed potatoes.

seafood stew

2 baby fennel bulbs (260g)
2 tablespoons lemon juice
1 tablespoon olive oil
2 medium brown onions (300g), chopped finely
4 cloves garlic, crushed
3 x 5cm (2¼ inch) thin strips orange rind
⅓ cup (80ml) dry white wine
1 teaspoon chilli flakes
pinch saffron threads
820g (26 ounces) canned diced tomatoes
1 litre (4 cups) fish stock
1 teaspoon white sugar
750g (1½ pounds) uncooked medium king prawns (shrimp)
750g (1½ pounds) small black mussels
750g (1½ pounds) skinless white fish fillets, cut into 3cm pieces

GARLIC CROÛTONS

675g (1¾ pounds) loaf sourdough bread, sliced thickly
3 cloves garlic, halved
2 tablespoons olive oil

1 Trim fennel; reserve fronds. Slice fennel as thinly as possible; combine with lemon juice in small bowl.

2 Heat oil in large saucepan; cook onion, stirring, until soft. Add garlic; cook, stirring, 1 minute.

3 Stir rind, wine, chilli and saffron into onion mixture; cook, stirring, 2 minutes. Add undrained tomatoes; simmer, uncovered, about 10 minutes or until mixture thickens slightly. Add stock; simmer, uncovered, about 20 minutes or until liquid is reduced by about a quarter. Stir in sugar.

4 Shell and devein prawns. Scrub mussels and remove beards.

5 Add prawns, mussels and fish to tomato mixture. Cover; simmer, stirring occasionally, about 5 minutes or until prawns change colour and mussels open (discard any that do not).

6 Meanwhile, make garlic croûtons.

7 Serve stew topped with garlic croûtons and fennel mixture; sprinkle over reserved fronds.

GARLIC CROÛTONS Toast bread both sides on heated grill plate (or grill or barbecue); rub one side of toast with cut garlic clove; drizzle with oil.

prep + cook time 1 hour **serves** 6
nutritional count per serving 17.2g total fat (3.5g saturated fat); 2792kJ (668 cal); 63.7g carbohydrate; 56.9g protein; 9.2g fibre

chicken cacciatore

2 tablespoons olive oil
1.5kg (3 pounds) chicken thigh cutlets, skin on
1 medium brown onion (150g), chopped finely
1 clove garlic, crushed
½ cup (125ml) dry white wine
2 tablespoons white wine vinegar
½ cup (125ml) chicken stock
410g (13 ounces) canned crushed tomatoes
¼ cup (70g) tomato paste
2 drained anchovy fillets, chopped finely
½ cup (60g) seeded black olives, chopped coarsely
½ cup coarsely chopped fresh flat-leaf parsley

1 Heat half the oil in large saucepan; cook chicken, in batches, until browned all over. Remove from pan.
2 Heat remaining oil in same pan; cook onion and garlic, stirring, until onion softens. Stir in wine, vinegar, stock, undrained tomatoes, paste and anchovies.
3 Return chicken to pan, fitting pieces tightly together in a single layer; bring to the boil. Reduce heat; simmer, covered, 20 minutes. Uncover; simmer about 30 minutes or until chicken is tender and sauce is reduced. Skim fat from surface; stir in olives and parsley.

prep + cook time 1 hours 30 minutes **serves** 4
nutritional count per serving 39.9g total fat (10.8g saturated fat); 2454kJ (587 cal); 10.8g carbohydrate; 40.5g protein; 3.1g fibre

chicken fricassee

45g (1½ ounces) butter
8 shallots (200g), peeled
20 baby carrots (400g), halved
1kg chicken thigh fillets, cut into thirds
2 tablespoons plain (all-purpose) flour
½ cup (125ml) dry white wine
1½ cups (375g) chicken stock
2 tablespoons dijon mustard
2 large kumara (orange sweet potato) (1kg), chopped coarsely
20g (¾ ounce) butter, extra
½ cup (125ml) pouring cream
2 egg yolks
¼ cup (60ml) pouring cream, extra
1 tablespoon lemon juice
2 tablespoons coarsely chopped fresh tarragon

1 Heat butter in large heavy-based saucepan; cook shallots and carrots, over low heat, stirring occasionally, about 5 minutes or until browned lightly, remove from pan. Cook chicken, in batches, in same pan, over low heat, until browned lightly. Remove from pan.
2 Add flour; cook, stirring, until mixture bubbles and thickens. Gradually stir in combined wine, stock and mustard. Return chicken to pan with shallots and carrots; bring to the boil. Simmer, covered, about 45 minutes or until chicken is cooked through.
3 Meanwhile, boil, steam or microwave kumara until tender; drain. Mash kumara with extra butter and cream in large bowl until smooth. Cover to keep warm.
4 Combine egg yolks, extra cream, juice and tarragon in medium jug. Remove fricassee from heat. Gradually add cream mixture, stirring constantly.
5 Serve fricassee with mash.

prep + cook time 1 hour 30 minutes **serves** 4
nutritional count per serving 54.1g total fat (27.9g saturated fat); 3825kJ (915 cal); 43.5g carbohydrate; 56.4g protein; 7.6g fibre

roasts

roast beef with yorkshire puddings

2kg (4 pounds) corned silverside (corner piece)
2 cups (500ml) dry red wine
2 bay leaves
6 black peppercorns
¼ cup (70g) wholegrain mustard
4 cloves garlic, sliced
4 sprigs fresh thyme
1 medium brown onion (150g), chopped coarsely
2 medium carrots (240g), chopped coarsely
1 large leek (500g), chopped coarsely
2 stalks celery (300g), trimmed, chopped coarsely
2 tablespoons olive oil

YORKSHIRE PUDDINGS
1 cup (150g) plain (all-purpose) flour
2 eggs
½ cup (125ml) milk
½ cup (125ml) water

GRAVY
2 tablespoons plain (all-purpose) flour
1½ cups (375ml) beef stock

1 Combine beef, wine, bay leaves, peppercorns, mustard, garlic, thyme and onion in large bowl, cover; refrigerate 3 hours or overnight.
2 Preheat oven to 180°C/350°F.
3 Drain beef over medium bowl; reserve 1 cup of marinade for gravy. Combine carrot, leek and celery in large baking dish, top with beef; brush beef with oil.
4 Roast beef, uncovered, about 1½ hours. Remove beef from dish, wrap in foil; stand 20 minutes.
5 Increase oven temperature to 220°C/425°F.
6 Remove vegetables from dish with slotted spoon; discard vegetables. Pour pan juices into jug; stand 2 minutes. Reserve 1½ tablespoons oil for yorkshire puddings, pour off excess oil; reserve 2 tablespoons of pan juices for gravy.
7 Make yorkshire puddings and gravy. Serve beef with yorkshire puddings and gravy.

YORKSHIRE PUDDINGS Sift flour into medium bowl; whisk in combined eggs, milk and water all at once until smooth. Stand batter 30 minutes. Divide the reserved oil among eight holes of 12-hole (⅓-cup/80ml) muffin pan; heat in oven 2 minutes. Divide batter among hot pan holes. Bake about 20 minutes or until puddings are puffed and golden.

GRAVY Heat reserved pan juices in same baking dish, add flour; cook, stirring, until browned. Gradually add stock and reserved marinade; cook, stirring, until mixture boils and thickens. Strain gravy into heatproof jug.

prep + cook time 2 hours 35 minutes (+ refrigeration and standing) **serves** 8
nutritional count per serving 15.4g total fat (4.8g saturated fat); 2169kJ (519 cal); 21.1g carbohydrate; 61.2g protein; 4g fibre

Serve with roast potatoes and steamed baby carrots.

roast turkey with forcemeat stuffing

4.5kg (9 pound) turkey
1 cup (250ml) water
75g (2½ ounces) butter, melted
¼ cup (35g) plain (all-purpose) flour
3 cups (750ml) chicken stock
½ cup (125ml) dry white wine
FORCEMEAT
45g (1½ ounces) butter
3 medium brown onions (450g), chopped finely
2 rindless bacon slices (130g), chopped coarsely
1 cup (70g) stale breadcrumbs
½ cup coarsely chopped fresh flat-leaf parsley
250g (8 ounces) minced (ground) pork
250g (8 ounces) minced (ground) chicken

1 Preheat oven to 180°C/350°F.
2 Make forcemeat.
3 Discard neck from turkey. Rinse turkey under cold water; pat dry inside and out with absorbent paper. Fill neck cavity loosely with forcemeat; secure skin over opening with small skewers. Fill large cavity loosely with forcemeat; tie legs together with kitchen string.
4 Place turkey on oiled wire rack in large shallow baking dish; pour the water into dish. Brush turkey all over with half the butter; cover turkey tightly with two layers of greased foil. Roast 2 hours.
5 Uncover turkey; brush with remaining butter. Roast turkey, uncovered, about 1 hour or until cooked through. Remove turkey from dish, cover loosely with foil; stand 20 minutes.
6 Pour juice from baking dish into large jug; skim 1 tablespoon of fat from juice, return fat to same dish. Skim and discard fat from remaining juice; reserve juice. Add flour to dish; cook, stirring, until mixture bubbles and is well-browned. Gradually stir in stock, wine and reserved juice; cook, stirring, until gravy boils and thickens. Strain gravy into jug; serve with turkey.
FORCEMEAT Melt butter in medium frying pan; cook onion and bacon, stirring, over low heat, until onion is soft, cool. Combine onion mixture and remaining ingredients in large bowl; season.

prep + cook time 3 hours 45 minutes (+ standing)
serves 8
nutritional count per serving 50.7g total fat (19.8g saturated fat); 3382kJ (809 cal); 12.8g carbohydrate; 72.9g protein; 1.4g fibre

roast lamb dinner

2kg (4 pound) leg of lamb
3 sprigs fresh rosemary, chopped coarsely
½ teaspoon sweet paprika
1kg (2 pounds) potatoes, chopped coarsely
500g (1 pound) piece pumpkin, chopped coarsely
3 small brown onions (240g), halved
2 tablespoons olive oil
2 tablespoons plain (all-purpose) flour
1 cup (250ml) chicken stock
¼ cup (60ml) dry red wine

1 Preheat oven to 200°C/400°F.
2 Place lamb in oiled large baking dish; using sharp knife, score skin at 2cm intervals, sprinkle with rosemary and paprika. Roast lamb 15 minutes.
3 Reduce oven temperature to 180°C/350°F; roast lamb a further 1 hour 15 minutes or until cooked as desired.
4 Meanwhile, place potatoes, pumpkin and onions, in single layer, in large shallow baking dish; drizzle with oil. Roast for last 45 minutes of lamb cooking time.
5 Remove lamb and vegetables from oven; strain pan juices from lamb into medium jug. Cover lamb and vegetables to keep warm. Return ¼ cup of the pan juices to baking dish, stir in flour; stir over heat about 5 minutes or until mixture bubbles and browns. Gradually add stock and wine; stir over high heat until gravy boils and thickens. Strain gravy into medium heatproof jug.
6 Slice lamb; serve with roasted vegetables and gravy.

prep + cook time 1 hour 40 minutes **serves** 6
nutritional count per serving 35.6g total fat (17g saturated fat); 3244kJ (776 cal); 40.5g carbohydrate; 71.9g protein; 7g fibre

Serve with cauliflower mornay.

roast chicken with herb stuffing

1.5kg (3 pound) whole chicken
20g (¾ ounce) butter, melted
HERB STUFFING
1½ cups (105g) stale breadcrumbs
1 stalk celery (150g), trimmed, chopped finely
1 small white onion (100g), chopped finely
1 teaspoon dried mixed herbs
1 egg, beaten lightly
45g (1½ ounces) butter, melted

1 Preheat oven to 200°C/400°F.
2 To make herb stuffing, combine ingredients in medium bowl.
3 Wash chicken under cold water; pat dry inside and out with absorbent paper. Fill cavity with stuffing, fold over skin to enclose; secure with toothpicks. Tie legs together with kitchen string.
4 Place chicken on rack over baking dish half-filled with water (water should not touch chicken). Brush chicken with melted butter; roast 15 minutes. Reduce oven temperature to 180°C/350°F; roast chicken about 1½ hours or until cooked through.
5 Stand chicken 10 minutes before serving.

prep + cook time 2 hours 15 minutes **serves** 4
nutritional count per serving 46.8g total fat (19.4g saturated fat); 2817kJ (674 cal); 19.7g carbohydrate; 43.4g protein; 1.9g fibre

Serve with steamed asparagus and roasted baby new potatoes.

herb-crumbed lamb racks

1 cup (70g) stale breadcrumbs
1 tablespoon finely chopped fresh flat-leaf parsley
2 tablespoons finely chopped fresh mint
2 teaspoons finely grated lemon rind
45g (1½ ounces) butter
2 shallots (50g), chopped finely
4 x 4 french-trimmed lamb cutlet racks (720g)
250g (8 ounces) baby vine-ripened truss tomatoes
cooking-oil spray

1 Preheat oven to 220°C/425°F.
2 Combine breadcrumbs, herbs and rind in small bowl.
3 Melt butter in small frying pan; pour half the butter into breadcrumb mixture.
4 Cook shallot in remaining butter, stirring, until soft; stir into breadcrumb mixture.
5 Place lamb and tomatoes in oiled large baking dish; spray tomatoes with oil. Press breadcrumb mixture onto lamb. Roast, uncovered, about 15 minutes or until cooked as desired. Serve lamb with roasted tomatoes.

prep + cook time 30 minutes **serves** 4
nutritional count per serving 25g total fat (12.6g saturated fat); 1538kJ (368 cal); 13.7g carbohydrate; 21.4g protein; 1.9g fibre

roast pork leg with sage potatoes

2.5kg (5 pound) boneless pork leg roast, rind on
2 tablespoons olive oil
1 tablespoon sea salt flakes
6 medium potatoes (1.2kg), quartered
2 tablespoons olive oil, extra
2 tablespoons fresh sage leaves
2 tablespoons fresh rosemary leaves

APPLE SAUCE
3 large green apples (600g)
¼ cup (60ml) water
1 teaspoon white sugar
pinch ground cinnamon

1 Preheat oven to 220°C/425°F.
2 Score pork rind with sharp knife; rub with oil, then salt. Place pork in large shallow baking dish. Roast, uncovered, 20 minutes.
3 Reduce oven temperature to 180°C/350°F. Roast, uncovered, about 2 hours.
4 Meanwhile, combine potato with extra oil and herbs in large bowl. Place, in single layer, on oven tray. Roast, uncovered, about 35 minutes.
5 Meanwhile, make apple sauce.
6 Stand pork, covered loosely with foil, 10 minutes before slicing. Serve pork and sage potatoes with apple sauce.

APPLE SAUCE Peel and core apples; slice thickly. Place apples and the water in medium saucepan; simmer, uncovered, about 10 minutes or until apple is soft. Remove pan from heat; stir in sugar and cinnamon.

prep + cook time 2 hours 40 minutes (+ standing)
serves 8
nutritional count per serving 34g total fat (9.7g saturated fat); 2976kJ (712 cal); 27.4g carbohydrate; 71.9g protein; 4.1g fibre

pasta

spaghetti and meatballs

250g (8 ounces) minced (ground) pork
250g (8 ounces) minced (ground) veal
½ cup (35g) stale breadcrumbs
1 egg
¼ cup (20g) finely grated parmesan cheese
1 tablespoon olive oil
1 medium brown onion (150g), chopped coarsely
2 cloves garlic, quartered
1 fresh small red thai chilli
6 anchovy fillets
1 cup (150g) drained sun-dried tomatoes in oil
¼ cup (70g) tomato paste
1 cup (250ml) chicken stock
12 pimiento-stuffed olives, sliced thinly
375g (12 ounces) spaghetti
⅓ cup coarsely chopped fresh flat-leaf parsley

1 Combine mince, breadcrumbs, egg and cheese in medium bowl; roll level tablespoons of mixture into balls.
2 Heat oil in medium frying pan; cook meatballs, uncovered, until browned.
3 Blend or process onion, garlic, chilli, anchovy, tomatoes and paste until smooth. Combine tomato mixture with stock in medium saucepan; bring to the boil. Add meatballs and olives to tomato mixture; simmer, uncovered, 15 minutes.
4 Meanwhile, cook spaghetti in large saucepan of boiling water until tender; drain.
5 Serve spaghetti topped with meatballs and sauce; sprinkle with parsley.

prep + cook time 50 minutes **serves** 4
nutritional count per serving 20.6g total fat (6.3g saturated fat); 2964kJ (709 cal); 78.8g carbohydrate; 47.5g protein; 7.9g fibre
note Some butchers sell a pork and veal mince mixture; you could buy 500g (1 pound) of this, if it's available.

spaghetti with pesto

2 cloves garlic, chopped coarsely
⅓ cup (50g) roasted pine nuts
½ cup (40g) finely grated parmesan cheese
2 cups firmly packed fresh basil leaves
½ cup (125ml) olive oil
500g (1 pound) spaghetti
½ cup (40g) flaked parmesan cheese

1 To make pesto, blend or process garlic, nuts, grated cheese and basil until almost smooth. Gradually add oil in a thin, steady stream, processing until thick.
2 Cook pasta in large saucepan of boiling water until just tender; drain, reserving ¼ cup of the cooking liquid.
3 Combine pasta, pesto and reserved cooking liquid in large bowl. Serve with flaked cheese.

prep + cook time 25 minutes **serves** 4
nutritional count per serving 45.2g total fat (8.9g saturated fat); 3578kJ (859 cal); 86.2g carbohydrate; 23.6g protein; 5.6g fibre

vegetarian lasagne

2 cups (500ml) bottled tomato pasta sauce
3 fresh lasagne sheets (150g)
¾ cup (110g) drained semi-dried tomatoes in oil, chopped coarsely
90g (3 ounce) piece fetta cheese, crumbled
½ cup (120g) firm ricotta cheese, crumbled
1½ cups (180g) coarsely grated cheddar cheese
1 cup (150g) drained marinated char-grilled eggplant, chopped coarsely
¾ cup (165g) drained char-grilled capsicum
125g (4 ounces) baby rocket leaves (arugula)

1 Preheat oven to 200°C/400°F.
2 Oil deep ovenproof dish (2.5-litre/10-cup). Spread ½ cup pasta sauce over base of dish; top with a lasagne sheet and another ½ cup pasta sauce. Top with semi-dried tomato, ¼ cup of each cheese, then another lasagne sheet. Top with ½ cup pasta sauce, eggplant, remaining fetta, remaining ricotta and another ¼ cup cheddar. Top with remaining lasagne sheet, remaining sauce and capsicum; sprinkle with remaining cheddar.
3 Bake lasagne, covered, 30 minutes. Uncover; bake 15 minutes. Stand 5 minutes before cutting; serve with rocket.

prep + cook time 55 minutes **serves** 4
nutritional count per serving 38.4g total fat (17.2g saturated fat); 2876kJ (688 cal); 49.6g carbohydrate; 31.4g protein; 9.9g fibre

fettuccine marinara

500g (1 pound) fresh fettuccine pasta
1 tablespoon olive oil
1 small brown onion (80g), chopped finely
2 tablespoons tomato paste
½ cup (125ml) dry white wine
3 cups (750ml) tomato pasta sauce
750g (1½ pounds) marinara mix
pinch saffron threads

1 Cook pasta in large saucepan of boiling water until tender; drain.
2 Heat oil in large saucepan; cook onion, stirring, until soft. Add paste; cook, stirring, 1 minute. Add wine; bring to the boil then reduce heat. Simmer, uncovered, 3 minutes.
3 Add sauce, marinara mix and saffron; bring to the boil then reduce heat. Simmer, uncovered, about 5 minutes or until seafood is cooked through. Serve pasta topped with sauce.

prep + cook time 30 minutes **serves** 4
nutritional count per serving 12.1g total fat (2.5g saturated fat); 3490kJ (835 cal); 104.3g carbohydrate; 66g protein; 7.9g fibre

spaghetti bolognese

2 teaspoons olive oil
6 slices pancetta (90g), chopped finely
1 large white onion (200g), chopped finely
1 medium carrot (120g), chopped finely
2 stalks celery (300g) trimmed, chopped finely
625g (1¼ pounds) minced (ground) beef
155g (5 ounces) chicken livers, trimmed, chopped finely
1 cup (250ml) milk
60g (2 ounces) butter
1½ cups (375ml) beef stock
1 cup (250ml) dry red wine
410g (13 ounces) canned tomato puree
2 tablespoons tomato paste
¼ cup finely chopped fresh flat-leaf parsley
750g (1½ pounds) fresh spaghetti
½ cup (40g) shaved parmesan cheese

1 Heat oil in large heavy-based frying pan; cook pancetta, stirring, until crisp. Add onion, carrot and celery; cook, stirring, until vegetables soften.
2 Add beef and liver to pan; cook, stirring, until beef changes colour. Stir in the milk and butter; cook, stirring occasionally, until liquid reduces to about half.
3 Add stock, wine, puree and paste to pan; simmer, covered, 1 hour. Uncover; simmer 1 hour. Remove from heat; stir in parsley.
4 Meanwhile, cook pasta in large saucepan of boiling water until tender; drain.
5 Serve pasta topped with sauce and cheese.

prep + cook time 2 hours 35 minutes **serves** 6
nutritional count per serving 26.6g total fat (13g saturated fat); 2504kJ (599 cal); 41g carbohydrate; 39.2g protein; 5.5g fibre

lasagne bolognese

2 teaspoons olive oil
6 slices pancetta (90g), chopped finely
1 large white onion (200g), chopped finely
1 medium carrot (120g), chopped finely
2 stalks celery (300g), trimmed, chopped finely
1kg (2 pounds) minced (ground) beef
155g (5 ounces) chicken livers, trimmed, chopped finely
2 cups (500ml) milk
60g butter
2 cups (500ml) beef stock
1 cup (250ml) dry red wine
410g (13 ounces) canned tomato puree
2 tablespoons tomato paste
¼ cup finely chopped fresh flat-leaf parsley
2 cups (160g) finely grated parmesan cheese

PASTA
1 cup (150g) plain (all-purpose) flour
¼ cup (45g) semolina flour
2 eggs
1 tablespoon olive oil
semolina flour, for dusting, extra

WHITE SAUCE
125g (4 ounces) butter
¾ cup (110g) plain (all-purpose) flour
1.25 litres (5 cups) hot milk

1 Heat oil in large heavy-based pan; cook pancetta, stirring, until crisp. Add onion, carrot and celery; cook, stirring, until vegetables soften. Add beef and liver; cook, stirring, until beef just changes colour. Stir in milk and butter; cook, stirring occasionally, until liquid reduces to about half. Add stock, wine, puree and paste; simmer, uncovered, 1½ hours. Remove from heat; stir in parsley.
2 Meanwhile, make pasta.
3 Preheat oven to 200°C/400°F. Grease deep 25cm x 35cm (10 inch x 14 inch) baking dish.
4 Make white sauce.
5 Spread ½ cup of the white sauce over base of dish. Layer two pasta sheets, a quarter of the meat sauce, ¼ cup of the cheese and 1 cup of the remaining white sauce in dish. Repeat the layering process, starting with pasta sheets and ending with white sauce; you will have four layers in total. Top lasagne with remaining cheese.
6 Bake lasagne about 40 minutes or until top is browned lightly. Stand 15 minutes before cutting.

PASTA Process flours, eggs and oil until mixture forms a ball. Knead dough on floured surface about 5 minutes or until smooth. Divide the dough into quarters; roll each piece through pasta machine set on thickest setting. Fold long sides of dough into the centre, roll through machine. Repeat rolling several times, adjusting setting so pasta sheets become thinner with each roll; dust pasta with extra semolina when necessary. Roll to second thinnest setting (1mm-thick), making sure pasta is at least 10cm (4 inches) wide. Cut pasta into 35cm (14 inch) lengths. Cook pasta in large saucepan of boiling water, in batches, about 1 minute or until pasta rises to the surface. Transfer to bowl of iced water; drain, pat dry with absorbent paper towel.

WHITE SAUCE Melt butter in medium saucepan, add flour; stir until mixture forms a smooth paste. Gradually stir in milk; bring to the boil, stirring, until sauce boils and thickens.

prep + cook time 4 hours (+ standing) **serves** 8
nutritional count per serving 53.2g total fat (29.1g saturated fat); 3720kJ (890 cal); 44.2g carbohydrate; 52.1g protein; 3.9g fibre

macaroni cheese

280g (9 ounces) macaroni pasta
4 rindless bacon slices (260g), chopped finely
45g (1½ ounces) butter
⅓ cup (50g) plain (all-purpose) flour
1 litre (4 cups) milk
1 cup (120g) coarsely grated cheddar cheese
½ cup (40g) finely grated pecorino cheese
2 tablespoons wholegrain mustard
½ cup (35g) stale breadcrumbs
20g (¾ ounce) butter, extra

1 Preheat oven to 180°C/350°F. Oil deep 2-litre (8-cup) ovenproof dish.
2 Cook pasta in large saucepan of boiling water until tender; drain.
3 Meanwhile, cook bacon in medium saucepan, stirring, until crisp; drain on absorbent paper.
4 Melt butter in same pan, add flour; cook, stirring, 1 minute. Gradually stir in milk; cook, stirring, until sauce boils and thickens. Cool 2 minutes; stir in cheeses and mustard.
5 Combine pasta, cheese sauce and bacon in large bowl; pour mixture into ovenproof dish. Top with breadcrumbs, dot with extra butter. Bake in oven, about 30 minutes or until browned.

prep + cook time 1 hour **serves** 4
nutritional count per serving 47.5g total fat (27.8g saturated fat); 3854kJ (922 cal); 78.8g carbohydrate; 43.1g protein; 3.5g fibre

penne puttanesca

500g (1 pound) penne pasta
4 whole anchovy fillets, drained
¼ cup (60ml) olive oil
1 fresh long red chilli, sliced thinly
3 cups (750ml) bottled tomato pasta sauce
1 cup (120g) seeded black olives
2 tablespoons drained, rinsed baby capers, chopped coarsely

1 Cook pasta in large saucepan of boiling water until tender; drain.
2 Finely chop anchovy fillets. Using side of heavy knife, press down firmly on anchovy to crush.
3 Heat 1 tablespoon of the oil in large saucepan; cook anchovy and chilli, stirring, 2 minutes. Add sauce; bring to the boil. Stir in olives, capers and remaining oil, reduce heat; simmer, uncovered, about 5 minutes or until heated through.
4 Serve pasta topped with sauce.

prep + cook time 30 minutes **serves** 4
nutritional count per serving 17.4g total fat (2.5g saturated fat); 2876kJ (687 cal); 107.4g carbohydrate; 20.4g protein; 7.7g fibre

gnocchi with three cheeses

1kg (2 pounds) potatoes, unpeeled
2 eggs, beaten lightly
30g (1 ounce) butter, melted
¼ cup (20g) finely grated parmesan cheese
2 cups (300g) plain (all-purpose) flour, approximately

THREE-CHEESE SAUCE
60g (2 ounces) butter
⅓ cup (50g) plain (all-purpose) flour
2 cups (500ml) milk
1¼ cups (310ml) pouring cream (see note)
60g (2 ounces) coarsely grated provolone cheese
75g (2½ ounces) coarsely grated fontina cheese
45g (1½ ounces) gorgonzola cheese, crumbled

1 Boil, steam or microwave whole potatoes until tender; drain. Peel when cool enough to handle. Mash potato using a ricer, or mouli, or push through a fine sieve with a wooden spoon into large bowl; stir in eggs, butter, parmesan and enough of the flour to make a firm dough.

2 Divide dough into eight equal portions; roll each portion on a lightly floured surface into 2cm (¾ inch) thick sausage shapes. Cut each sausage shape into 2cm (¾ inch) pieces; roll pieces into balls.

3 Roll each ball along the tines of a fork, pressing lightly on top of ball with index finger to form the classic gnocchi shape – grooves on one side and a dimple on the other. Place gnocchi, in single layer, on lightly floured tray, cover; refrigerate 1 hour.

4 Meanwhile, make three-cheese sauce.

5 Cook gnocchi in large saucepan of boiling water, uncovered, about 3 minutes or until gnocchi float to the surface. Remove from pan with slotted spoon; drain. Serve gnocchi topped with sauce.

THREE-CHEESE SAUCE Melt butter in medium saucepan, add flour; cook, stirring, until mixture bubbles and thickens. Gradually stir in milk and cream until mixture boils and thickens. Remove from heat; stir in cheeses.

prep + cook time 1 hour 10 minutes (+ refrigeration)
serves 8
nutritional count per serving 37.5g total fat (23.8g saturated fat); 2638kJ (631 cal); 52.2g carbohydrate; 19.5g protein; 4.2g fibre
note It is fine to use 1 x 300ml carton of cream for this recipe.

pastitsio

250g (8 ounces) macaroni pasta
2 eggs, beaten lightly
¾ cup (60g) coarsely grated parmesan cheese
2 tablespoons stale breadcrumbs

MEAT SAUCE
2 tablespoons olive oil
2 medium brown onions (300g), chopped finely
750g (1½ pounds) minced (ground) beef
410g (13 ounces) canned crushed tomatoes
⅓ cup (90g) tomato paste
½ cup (125ml) beef stock
¼ cup (60ml) dry white wine
½ teaspoon ground cinnamon
1 egg, beaten lightly

CHEESE TOPPING
90g (3 ounces) butter
½ cup (75g) plain (all-purpose) flour
3½ cups (875ml) milk
1 cup (80g) coarsely grated parmesan cheese
2 egg yolks

1 Preheat oven to 180°C/350°F. Oil shallow 2.5-litre (10-cup) ovenproof dish.
2 Make meat sauce; make cheese topping.
3 Cook pasta in large saucepan of boiling water until tender; drain. Combine hot pasta, egg and cheese in large bowl. Press pasta over base of dish.
4 Top pasta evenly with meat sauce; pour over cheese topping. Smooth surface; sprinkle with breadcrumbs. Bake, in oven, about 1 hour or until browned lightly. Stand 10 minutes before serving.

MEAT SAUCE Heat oil in large saucepan, add onion and beef; cook, stirring, until beef is browned. Stir in undrained tomatoes, paste, stock, wine and cinnamon; simmer, uncovered, about 20 minutes or until mixture is thick. Cool; stir in egg.

CHEESE TOPPING Melt butter in medium saucepan, add flour; cook, stirring, until mixture bubbles and thickens. Remove from heat; gradually stir in milk. Stir over heat until sauce boils and thickens; stir in cheese. Cool 5 minutes; stir in egg yolks.

prep + cook time 2 hours 15 minutes **serves** 6
nutritional count per serving 45.8g total fat (22.7g saturated fat); 3528kJ (844 cal); 52.5g carbohydrate; 52.1g protein; 4.1g fibre

spinach and ricotta cannelloni

1kg (2 pounds) spinach, trimmed, chopped coarsely
500g (1 pound) ricotta cheese
2 eggs
1½ cups (120g) coarsely grated parmesan cheese
¼ cup finely chopped fresh mint
2 teaspoons finely chopped fresh thyme
2 teaspoons finely chopped fresh rosemary
250g (8 ounces) cannelloni tubes
CREAMY TOMATO SAUCE
1 tablespoon olive oil
1 medium brown onion (150g), chopped finely
4 cloves garlic, crushed
1.6kg (56 ounces) canned diced tomatoes
½ cup (125ml) pouring cream
1 teaspoon white sugar

1 Make creamy tomato sauce.
2 Meanwhile, preheat oven to 180°C/350°F.
3 Cook washed, drained spinach in heated large saucepan, stirring, until wilted. Drain; when cool enough to handle, squeeze out excess moisture.
4 Combine spinach in large bowl with ricotta, eggs, ½ cup of the parmesan cheese and the herbs. Using a large piping bag, fill pasta with spinach mixture.
5 Spread a third of the sauce into shallow 25cm x 35cm (10 inch x 14 inch) ovenproof dish; top with pasta tubes, in single layer, then top with remaining sauce. Cook, covered, in oven, 20 minutes. Uncover, sprinkle pasta with remaining parmesan; cook about 15 minutes or until pasta is tender and cheese is browned lightly.

CREAMY TOMATO SAUCE Heat oil in large saucepan; cook onion, stirring, until softened. Add garlic; cook, stirring, until fragrant. Add undrained tomatoes; bring to the boil. Reduce heat; simmer, uncovered, stirring occasionally, about 20 minutes or until sauce thickens slightly. Cool 10 minutes; blend or process sauce with cream and sugar until smooth.

prep + cook time 1 hour **serves** 6
nutritional count per serving 31g total fat (17.1g saturated fat); 2412kJ (577 cal); 41.8g carbohydrate; 28.7g protein; 8.3g fibre

stir-fries

chicken, mixed vegie and almond stir-fry

2½ cups (500g) jasmine rice
2 tablespoons peanut oil
625g (1¼ pounds) chicken breast fillets, sliced thinly
1 medium brown onion (150g), sliced thinly
2 cloves garlic, crushed
345g (11 ounces) broccolini, trimmed, chopped coarsely
125g (4 ounces) fresh baby corn, halved lengthways
155g (5 ounces) sugar snap peas, trimmed
⅓ cup (45g) roasted slivered almonds
1 tablespoon fish sauce
1 tablespoon sweet chilli sauce

1 Cook rice in large saucepan of boiling water until just tender; drain. Cover to keep warm.
2 Meanwhile, heat half the oil in wok; stir-fry chicken, in batches, until browned lightly and cooked through. Remove from wok.
3 Heat remaining oil in wok; stir-fry onion and garlic until onion softens. Add broccolini, corn and peas; stir-fry until vegetables are tender.
4 Return chicken to wok with nuts and sauces; stir-fry until heated through. Serve with rice.

prep + cook time 35 minutes **serves** 4
nutritional count per serving 20.2g total fat (3.1g saturated fat); 3515kJ (841 cal); 109.4g carbohydrate; 50.5g protein; 7.5g fibre

sesame chicken stir-fry

345g (11 ounces) bean thread vermicelli
1 tablespoon peanut oil
2 chicken breast fillets (400g), sliced thinly
1 medium brown onion (150g), sliced thinly
1 clove garlic, crushed
280g (9 ounces) broccolini, chopped coarsely
2 tablespoons fish sauce
1 tablespoon hot chilli sauce (see note)
2 tablespoons dark soy sauce
1 tablespoon toasted sesame seeds
1 fresh long red chilli, chopped finely
4 green onions (scallions), sliced thinly
1 cup (80g) bean sprouts

1 Place vermicelli in medium heatproof bowl, cover with boiling water; stand until just tender, drain.
2 Meanwhile, heat half the oil in wok; stir-fry chicken, in batches, until browned. Remove from wok.
3 Heat remaining oil in wok; stir-fry brown onion, garlic and broccolini until onion softens.
4 Return chicken to wok with vermicelli, combined sauces, sesame seeds and half the chilli, half the green onion and half the sprouts; stir-fry just until heated through.
5 Serve stir-fry topped with remaining chilli, green onion and sprouts.

prep + cook time 40 minutes **serves** 4
nutritional count per serving 9.3g total fat (1.6g saturated fat); 1325kJ (317 cal); 23.9g carbohydrate; 31.3g protein; 5.6g fibre
note Use a mild chilli sauce, or omit altogether if you are unable to tolerate hot chilli.

sang chow bow

2 teaspoons sesame oil
1 small brown onion (80g), chopped finely
2 cloves garlic, crushed
2cm (¾ inch) piece fresh ginger (10g), grated
500g (1 pound) minced (ground) pork
2 tablespoons water
125g (4 ounces) shiitake mushrooms, chopped finely
2 tablespoons light soy sauce
2 tablespoons oyster sauce
1 tablespoon lime juice
2 cups (160g) bean sprouts
4 green onions (scallions), sliced thinly
¼ cup coarsely chopped fresh coriander (cilantro)
12 large butter (boston) lettuce leaves

1 Heat oil in wok; stir-fry brown onion, garlic and ginger until onion softens. Add pork; stir-fry until changed in colour.
2 Add the water, mushrooms, sauces and juice to wok; stir-fry until mushrooms are tender. Remove from heat. Add sprouts, green onion and coriander; toss to combine.
3 Spoon sang choy bow into lettuce leaves to serve.

prep + cook time 30 minutes **serves** 4
nutritional count per serving 11.5g total fat (3.6g saturated fat); 1112kJ (266 cal); 8.9g carbohydrate; 29.3g protein; 4.1g fibre

beef chow mein

1 tablespoon vegetable oil
500g (1 pound) minced (ground) beef
1 medium brown onion (150g), chopped finely
2 cloves garlic, crushed
1 tablespoon curry powder
1 large carrot (180g), chopped finely
2 stalks celery (300g), trimmed, sliced thinly
155g (5 ounces) button mushrooms, sliced thinly
1 cup (250ml) chicken stock
⅓ cup (80ml) oyster sauce
2 tablespoons dark soy sauce
440g (14 ounces) thin fresh egg noodles
½ cup (60g) frozen peas
½ wombok (napa cabbage) (350g), shredded coarsely

1 Heat oil in wok; stir-fry beef, onion and garlic until beef is browned. Add curry powder; stir-fry about 1 minute or until fragrant. Add carrot, celery and mushrooms; stir-fry until vegetables soften.
2 Add stock, sauces and noodles to wok; stir-fry 2 minutes. Add peas and cabbage; stir-fry until cabbage just wilts.

prep + cook time 50 minutes **serves** 4
nutritional count per serving 15.7g total fat (4.6g saturated fat); 2571kJ (615 cal); 70.6g carbohydrate; 42.3g protein; 8.4g fibre

sweet and sour pork

750g (1½ pounds) pork fillet, sliced thinly
1 tablespoon sweet sherry
½ cup (125ml) light soy sauce
¾ cup (110g) plain (all-purpose) flour
vegetable oil, for deep-frying
1 tablespoon vegetable oil, extra
1 medium red onion (170g), chopped coarsely
2 cloves garlic, crushed
1 medium red capsicum (bell pepper) (200g), chopped coarsely
1 medium green capsicum (bell pepper) (200g), chopped coarsely
1 medium carrot (120g), sliced thinly
500g (1 pound) fresh pineapple, chopped coarsely
155g (5 ounces) sugar snap peas, trimmed
⅓ cup (80ml) chicken stock
¼ cup (70g) tomato sauce
¼ cup (60ml) white vinegar
¼ cup (55g) white sugar
½ cup loosely packed fresh coriander (cilantro) leaves

1 Combine pork with sherry and 2 tablespoons of the soy sauce in medium bowl; coat pork in flour, shake off excess.
2 Heat oil in wok; deep-fry pork, in batches, until browned and crisp. Remove from wok; drain on absorbent paper. (Strain oil, save for another use.)
3 Heat extra oil in wok; stir-fry onion and garlic until onion softens. Add capsicums and carrot; stir-fry until vegetables are tender. Return pork to wok with pineapple, peas, remaining soy sauce, stock, tomato sauce, vinegar and sugar; stir-fry until hot. Remove from heat; stir in coriander.

prep + cook time 40 minutes **serves** 4
nutritional count per serving 20.2g total fat (3.6g saturated fat); 2717kJ (650 cal); 57.7g carbohydrate; 53.7g protein; 7.5g fibre

garlic and chilli seafood stir-fry

750g (1½ pounds) uncooked medium king prawns (shrimp)
2 cleaned squid hoods (300g)
500g (1 pound) octopus, quartered
¼ cup (60ml) peanut oil
6 cloves garlic, sliced thinly
2cm (¾ inch) piece fresh ginger (10g), sliced thinly
2 fresh long red chillies, sliced thinly
2 tablespoons chinese cooking wine
1 teaspoon caster (superfine) sugar
4 green onions (scallions), cut in 4cm (1½ inch) pieces

CHILLI FRIED SHALLOTS
1 tablespoon fried shallots
1 teaspoon sea salt flakes
½ teaspoon dried chilli flakes

1 Shell and devein prawns, leaving tails intact. Cut squid down centre to open out; score inside in a diagonal pattern, then cut into thick strips. Quarter octopus lengthways.
2 Combine ingredients for chilli fried shallots in small bowl.
3 Heat 1 tablespoon of the oil in wok; stir-fry prawns until changed in colour, remove from wok. Heat another tablespoon of the oil in wok; stir-fry squid until cooked through, remove from wok. Heat remaining oil in wok; stir-fry octopus until tender, remove from wok.
4 Stir-fry garlic, ginger and chilli in wok until fragrant. Return seafood to wok with remaining ingredients; stir-fry until hot.
5 Serve stir-fry sprinkled with chilli fried shallots.

prep + cook time 45 minutes **serves** 4
nutritional count per serving 4.7g total fat (0.8g saturated fat); 460kJ (110 cal); 0.8g carbohydrate; 15.5g protein; 0.3g fibre

mixed green vegetables and fried tofu

315g (10 ounces) fresh firm silken tofu
1 tablespoon peanut oil
1 medium brown onion (150g), sliced thinly
2 cloves garlic, crushed
2cm (¾ inch) piece fresh ginger (10g), grated
1 fresh small red thai chilli, chopped finely
345g (11 ounces) asparagus, cut into 3cm lengths
345g (11 ounces) broccolini, cut into 3cm lengths
200g (6½ ounces) sugar snap peas, trimmed
500g (1 pound) buk choy, chopped coarsely
¼ cup (60ml) vegetable stock
¼ cup (60ml) hoisin sauce
¼ cup (60ml) vegetarian mushroom oyster sauce
1 tablespoon lime juice
90g (3 ounces) bean sprouts

1 Cut tofu into 2cm (¾ inch) cubes; spread, in single layer, on absorbent-paper-lined tray. Cover tofu with more absorbent paper, stand 10 minutes.
2 Heat half the oil in wok; stir-fry tofu, in batches, until browned lightly. Remove from wok.
3 Heat remaining oil in wok; stir-fry onion, garlic, ginger and chilli until onion softens. Add asparagus, broccolini and peas; stir-fry until vegetables are tender. Add buk choy, stock, sauces and juice; stir-fry until buk choy wilts.
4 Return tofu to wok; stir-fry until combined. Remove from heat; stir in sprouts.

prep + cook time 35 minutes **serves** 4
nutritional count per serving 11.6g total fat (1.8g saturated fat); 1191kJ (285 cal); 18.4g carbohydrate; 20.5g protein; 12.3g fibre

combination fried rice

315g (10 ounces) uncooked small king prawns (shrimp)
¼ cup (60ml) peanut oil
410g (13 ounces) chicken breast fillets, sliced thinly
3 eggs, beaten lightly
4 rindless bacon slices (260g), chopped coarsely
1 medium brown onion (150g), chopped finely
1 medium red capsicum (bell pepper) (200g), chopped finely
2 cloves garlic, crushed
2.5cm (1 inch) piece fresh ginger (15g), grated
3 cups cooked white long-grain rice (see note)
2 tablespoons light soy sauce
¾ cup (90g) frozen peas
3 green onions (scallions), sliced thinly

1 Shell and devein prawns, leaving tails intact.
2 Heat 1 tablespoon of the oil in wok; stir-fry chicken, in batches, until cooked. Remove from wok. Stir-fry prawns in wok, in batches, until changed in colour; remove from wok.
3 Heat half the remaining oil in wok; stir-fry egg until just set then remove from wok.
4 Heat remaining oil in wok; stir-fry bacon, brown onion, capsicum, garlic and ginger until bacon is crisp. Return chicken, prawns and egg to wok with remaining ingredients; stir-fry until hot.

prep + cook time 40 minutes **serves** 4
nutritional count per serving 35.1g total fat (9.4g saturated fat); 3001kJ (718 cal); 46.5g carbohydrate; 52.3g protein; 3.9g fibre
note You need to cook 1⅓ cups of white long-grain rice the day before you make this dish; spread the cooled rice on a tray, cover and refrigerate overnight.

singapore noodles

440g (14 ounces) fresh singapore noodles
2 teaspoons sesame oil
2 cloves garlic, crushed
2cm (¾ inch) piece fresh ginger (10g), grated
1 medium carrot (120g), cut into matchsticks
250g (8 ounces) cooked shelled small prawns (shrimp)
1 tablespoon malaysian curry powder
3 green onions (scallions), sliced thinly
1½ cups (120g) bean sprouts
2 tablespoons japanese soy sauce
¼ cup (60ml) kecap manis
3 cups (480g) shredded barbecued chicken

1 Place noodles in large heatproof bowl, cover with boiling water; separate with fork, drain.
2 Meanwhile, heat oil in wok; stir-fry garlic, ginger and carrot until carrot is just tender. Add prawns and curry powder; stir-fry until prawns change colour.
3 Add noodles and remaining ingredients to wok; stir-fry until hot.

prep + cook time 25 minutes **serves** 4
nutritional count per serving 19.1g total fat (6.4g saturated fat); 2057kJ (492 cal); 27.3g carbohydrate; 49.1g protein; 5.8g fibre

eggs

boiled eggs

4 eggs

1 Place eggs in medium saucepan; add enough cold water to cover eggs. Stir constantly using a wooden spoon over high heat until water boils; this will centralise each yolk.
2 Boil, uncovered, until yolks are as soft or as firm as you like. As a guide, 3 minutes will give you set egg white and soft yolk. After 5 minutes, the yolk will be set.
3 Place saucepan of eggs under cold running water about 1 minute or until eggs are cool. This will stop a dark ring forming around the yolk.

prep + cook time 10 minutes **makes** 4
nutritional count per egg 5.3g total fat (1.6g saturated fat); 309kJ (74 cal); 0.2g carbohydrate; 6.7g protein; 0g fibre

poached eggs

2 teaspoons white vinegar
4 eggs

1 Half-fill a large shallow frying pan with water; add vinegar. Bring to the boil.
2 Break 1 egg into a cup or small bowl. Swirl the boiling water with a spoon, then slide egg into pan. Repeat with three more eggs. When all eggs are in pan, allow water to return to the boil.
3 Cover pan, turn off heat; stand about 4 minutes or until a light film of egg white sets over yolks.
4 Remove eggs with a slotted spoon and drain on absorbent paper.

prep + cook time 10 minutes **makes** 4
nutritional count per egg 5.3g total fat (1.6g saturated fat); 309kJ (74 cal); 0.2g carbohydrate; 6.7g protein; 0g fibre

poached eggs

gruyère soufflé

⅓ cup (50g) plain (all-purpose) flour
1⅔ cups (410ml) milk
20g (¾ ounce) butter, chopped
6 eggs, separated
1⅓ cups (165g) grated gruyère cheese
90g (3 ounces) sliced smoked salmon
1½ teaspoons rinsed, drained baby capers
1 tablespoon fresh chervil leaves

1 Preheat oven to 200°C/400°F. Grease 2-litre (8-cup) ovenproof soufflé dish. Place dish on oven tray.
2 Place flour in small saucepan; gradually whisk in the milk until a smooth paste forms. Cook flour mixture over medium heat, whisking constantly, until the mixture boils and thickens. Remove from heat. Stir in butter.
3 Whisk egg yolks and cheese into flour mixture; transfer to large bowl.
4 Beat egg whites in large bowl with electric mixer until soft peaks form. Fold egg whites into cheese mixture in two batches.
5 Pour mixture into dish; bake about 35 minutes or until soufflé is well risen and browned.
6 Meanwhile, arrange salmon on serving platter, top with the capers and chervil.
7 Serve soufflé immediately with the salmon.

prep + cook time 55 minutes **serves** 4
nutritional count per serving 29.6g total fat (15.8g saturated fat); 1881kJ (450 cal); 14.4g carbohydrate; 31.7g protein; 0.5g fibre

creamy scrambled eggs

8 eggs
½ cup (125ml) pouring cream
2 tablespoons finely chopped fresh chives
30g (1 ounce) butter

1 Place eggs, cream and chives in medium bowl; beat lightly with a fork.
2 Heat butter in large frying pan over medium heat. Add egg mixture, wait a few seconds, then use a wide spatula to gently scrape the set egg mixture along the base of the pan; cook until creamy and barely set. Serve immediately, with toast, if you like.

prep + cook time 20 minutes **serves** 4
nutritional count per serving 30.2g total fat (16.2g saturated fat); 1375kJ (329 cal); 1.3g carbohydrate; 14g protein; 0g fibre

herb omelette with sautéed mushrooms

2 tablespoons finely chopped fresh flat-leaf parsley
2 tablespoons finely chopped fresh chervil
2 tablespoons finely chopped fresh chives
2 tablespoons finely chopped fresh tarragon
45g (1½ ounces) butter
2 tablespoons olive oil
250g (8 ounces) swiss brown mushrooms, halved
½ cup (125ml) water
2 teaspoons finely grated lemon rind
1 tablespoon lemon juice
12 eggs

1 Combine herbs in small bowl.
2 Heat 30g of the butter and 1 tablespoon of the oil in large frying pan. Add mushrooms; cook, stirring, 5 minutes. Stir in 2 tablespoons of the water; cook, stirring, until water evaporates and mushrooms are tender. Remove from heat; stir in rind, juice and 2 tablespoons of the herb mixture. Cover to keep warm.
3 Gently whisk eggs and remaining water in large bowl; whisk in remaining herb mixture.
4 Heat a quarter of the remaining butter and 1 teaspoon of the remaining oil in medium frying pan. When butter mixture bubbles, pour a quarter of the egg mixture into pan; cook over medium heat, tilting pan, until egg is almost set. Tilt pan backwards; fold omelette in half. Cook 30 seconds then slide onto serving plate.
5 Repeat step 4, wiping out pan before each addition, to make a total of 4 omelettes. Serve omelettes topped with sautéed mushrooms.

prep + cook time 30 minutes **serves** 4
nutritional count per serving 35.3g total fat (12.9g saturated fat); 1718kJ (411 cal); 1g carbohydrate; 22.5g protein; 2g fibre

potato frittata

20g (¾ ounce) butter
1 tablespoon olive oil
2 medium potatoes (400g), cut into 1cm pieces
1 green onion (scallion), chopped finely
8 eggs
¼ cup (60ml) pouring cream
⅓ cup (25g) finely grated parmesan cheese
1 tablespoon finely chopped fresh dill
200g (6½ ounces) smoked salmon
2 tablespoons sour cream

1 Preheat oven to 220°C/425°F.
2 Heat butter and oil in 18cm (6¾ inch) medium ovenproof frying pan; cook potato, stirring occasionally, until browned and tender. Add onion; cook, stirring gently, 1 minute.
3 Meanwhile, whisk eggs, cream, cheese and dill in medium jug. Pour into pan; stir gently. Cook frittata over medium heat, about 2 minutes or until bottom sets. Place pan in oven; cook, uncovered, about 10 minutes or until frittata sets.
4 Slide frittata onto serving plate; serve topped with salmon, sour cream and extra dill, if you like.

prep + cook time 25 minutes **serves** 4
nutritional count per serving 34.1g total fat (15.2g saturated fat); 2031kJ (486 cal); 14.3g carbohydrate; 30.2g protein; 2.1g fibre

eggs benedict

8 eggs
4 english muffins
200g (6½ ounces) shaved leg ham
¼ cup finely chopped fresh chives
HOLLANDAISE SAUCE
1½ tablespoons white wine vinegar
1 tablespoon lemon juice
½ teaspoon black peppercorns
2 egg yolks
125g (4 ounces) unsalted butter, melted

1 Make hollandaise sauce.
2 To poach eggs, half-fill a large shallow frying pan with water; bring to the boil. Break 1 egg into a cup, then slide into pan; repeat with three more eggs. When all eggs are in pan, allow water to return to the boil. Cover pan, turn off heat; stand about 4 minutes or until a light film of egg white sets over yolks. Remove eggs with a slotted spoon; drain on absorbent paper, cover to keep warm. Repeat with remaining eggs.
3 Meanwhile, split muffins in half and toast. Serve muffins topped with ham, poached eggs, sauce and chives.

HOLLANDAISE SAUCE Combine vinegar, juice and peppercorns in small saucepan; bring to the boil. Reduce heat; simmer, uncovered, until liquid is reduced by half. Strain through a fine sieve into small heatproof bowl; cool 10 minutes. Whisk egg yolks into vinegar mixture. Set bowl over small saucepan of simmering water; do not allow water to touch base of bowl. Whisk mixture over heat until thickened. Remove bowl from heat; gradually whisk in melted butter in a thin steady stream, whisking constantly until sauce is thick and creamy.

prep + cook time 50 minutes **serves** 4
nutritional count per serving 40.6g total fat (21.2g saturated fat); 2450kJ (586 cal); 24.2g carbohydrate; 30.8g protein; 2g fibre

egg-white omelette

12 egg whites
4 green onions (scallions), chopped finely
¼ cup finely chopped fresh chives
¼ cup finely chopped fresh chervil
½ cup finely chopped fresh flat-leaf parsley
½ cup (60g) coarsely grated cheddar cheese
½ cup (50g) coarsely grated mozzarella cheese

1 Preheat grill (broiler).
2 Beat a quarter of the egg white in small bowl with electric mixer until soft peaks form; fold in a quarter of the combined onion and herbs.
3 Pour mixture into 20cm heated oiled frying pan; cook, uncovered, over low heat until omelette is just browned lightly on the bottom.
4 Sprinkle a quarter of the combined cheeses over half the omelette. Grill until cheese begins to melt and omelette sets; fold omelette over to completely cover cheese. Carefully slide onto serving plate; cover to keep warm.
5 Repeat to make 3 more omelettes.

prep + cook time 45 minutes **serves** 4
nutritional count per serving 7.9g total fat (5g saturated fat); 620kJ (148 cal); 1.1g carbohydrate; 18.2g protein; g fibre

spanish omelette

2 large potatoes (600g), sliced thinly
2 medium brown onions (300g), sliced thinly
155g (5 ounces) green beans, trimmed, chopped coarsely
1 medium red capsicum (bell pepper) (200g), chopped coarsely
8 eggs
¼ cup (60ml) skim milk
¼ cup coarsely chopped fresh flat-leaf parsley

TOMATO SALSA

1 large tomato (220g), seeded, chopped finely
2 lebanese cucumbers (260g), seeded, chopped finely
1 small red onion (100g), chopped finely
2 long green chillies, chopped finely
¼ cup (60ml) lemon juice
2 tablespoons finely chopped fresh coriander (cilantro)

1 Heat oiled 25cm (10 inch) frying pan; cook potato and onion, stirring, 2 minutes. Reduce heat; cook, covered, stirring occasionally, 15 minutes. Add beans and capsicum; cook, covered, about 5 minutes or until potato is tender. Remove from heat.
2 Whisk eggs, milk and parsley in large jug. Pour over potato mixture; stir gently.
3 Return pan to low heat; cook, uncovered, 20 minutes. Cover; cook about 10 minutes or until omelette is cooked.
4 Meanwhile, combine ingredients for tomato salsa in small bowl.
5 Serve omelette topped with salsa.

prep + cook time 1 hour 10 minutes **serves** 6
nutritional count per serving 7.4g total fat (2.2g saturated fat); 1672kJ (200 cal); 18.7g carbohydrate; 14.1g protein; 4.5g fibre

quiche lorraine

1 medium brown onion (150g), chopped finely
3 rindless bacon slices (195g), chopped finely
3 eggs
1¼ cups (310ml) pouring cream (see note)
½ cup (125ml) milk
¾ cup (120g) coarsely grated gruyère cheese
PASTRY
1¾ cups (260g) plain (all-purpose) flour
155g (5 ounces) cold butter, chopped coarsely
1 egg yolk
2 teaspoons lemon juice
⅓ cup (80ml) iced water, approximately

1 Make pastry.
2 Preheat oven to 200°C/400°F.
3 Roll pastry between sheets of baking paper until large enough to line a deep 23cm loose-based flan tin. Lift pastry into tin; gently press pastry around side. Trim edge, place tin on oven tray. Cover pastry with baking paper; fill with dried beans or rice. Bake 10 minutes; remove paper and beans. Bake pastry a further 10 minutes or until golden brown; cool.
4 Reduce oven temperature to 180°C/350°F.
5 Cook onion and bacon in heated oiled small frying pan until onion is soft; drain on absorbent paper, cool. Sprinkle bacon mixture over pastry case.
6 Whisk eggs in medium bowl then whisk in cream, milk and cheese; pour into pastry case. Bake, in oven, about 35 minutes or until filling is set. Stand 5 minutes before removing quiche from tin.
PASTRY Sift flour into bowl; rub in butter. Add egg yolk, juice and enough of the water to make ingredients cling together. Knead gently on lightly floured surface until smooth; cover, refrigerate 30 minutes.

prep + cook time 1 hour 30 minutes (+ refrigeration)
serves 6
nutritional count per serving 51.8g total fat (35.4g saturated fat); 3139kJ (751 cal); 35.4g carbohydrate; 22.1g protein; 2g fibre
note It is fine to use 1 x 300ml carton of cream for this recipe.

sauces

béchamel

30g (1 ounce) butter
2 tablespoons plain (all-purpose) flour
1¼ cups (310ml) hot milk
pinch nutmeg

1 Melt butter in medium saucepan, add flour; cook, stirring, until mixture bubbles and thickens. Gradually add milk, stirring, until mixture boils and thickens. Stir nutmeg into sauce.

prep + cook time 20 minutes **makes** 1 cup
nutritional count per tablespoon 3.1g total fat (2.1g saturated fat); 176kJ (42 cal); 2.6g carbohydrate; 1.1g protein; 0.1g fibre
notes Use in pasta dishes like lasagne, or serve with grilled fish fillets or corned beef. Béchamel is the base for many other sauces, including mornay (see recipe, page 111).

basic tomato pasta sauce

2 tablespoons olive oil
1 small brown onion (80g), chopped finely
1 clove garlic, crushed
2kg (4 pounds) ripe tomatoes, peeled, seeded, chopped coarsely
⅓ cup loosely packed fresh basil leaves

1 Heat oil in large saucepan; cook onion and garlic, stirring, until onion softens.
2 Add tomato and basil; cook, stirring, 5 minutes or until tomato begins to soften. Bring to the boil. Reduce heat; simmer, uncovered, stirring occasionally, about 40 minutes or until sauce thickens.

prep + cook time 1 hour **makes** 2 cups
nutritional count per ¼ cup 4.8g total fat (0.6g saturated fat); 343kJ (82 cal); 5.4g carbohydrate; 2.7g protein; 3.3g fibre
note Serve over cooked pasta.

mint sauce

2 cups firmly packed fresh mint leaves
¼ cup (60ml) water
¾ cup (180ml) white wine vinegar
2 tablespoons caster (superfine) sugar

1 Chop half the mint coarsely; place in a small heatproof bowl.
2 Combine the water, vinegar and sugar in small saucepan; stir over heat, without boiling, until sugar dissolves. Pour liquid over chopped mint in bowl, cover; stand 3 hours.
3 Strain liquid into bowl; discard mint. Chop remaining mint coarsely; stir into liquid. Blend or process until chopped finely.

prep + cook time 10 minutes (+ standing)
makes 1 cup
nutritional count per tablespoon 0.3g total fat (0.1g saturated fat); 234kJ (56 cal); 10.1g carbohydrate; 0.9g protein; 1.9g fibre
note Mint sauce is the classic accompaniment to serve with roast lamb.

rich gravy

2 teaspoons olive oil
1kg (2 pound) piece beef sirloin
2 medium carrots (240g), chopped coarsely
4 shallots (100g), quartered
2 stalks celery (300g), trimmed, chopped coarsely
2 teaspoons plain (all-purpose) flour
1 tablespoon tomato paste
2 cups (500ml) beef stock
1 cup (250ml) water

1 Preheat oven to 200°C/400°F.
2 Heat oil in large flameproof casserole dish; cook beef, uncovered, over high heat on stove top, until browned. Transfer to oven; roast, uncovered, about 45 minutes or until beef is cooked as desired.
3 Remove beef from dish; cover to keep warm.
4 To make gravy, place dish with pan juices over high heat, add carrot, shallot and celery; cook, uncovered, stirring occasionally, about 10 minutes or until vegetables are well-browned. Add flour; cook, stirring, about 4 minutes or until mixture is dark brown. Add paste, stock and the water; bring to the boil. Boil, uncovered, about 10 minutes or until gravy thickens.
5 Strain sauce, discard vegetables. Slice beef; serve with gravy.

prep + cook time 1 hour 25 minutes **serves** 4
nutritional count per serving 20.2g total fat (8.2g saturated fat); 1789kJ (428 cal); 6.5g carbohydrate; 53.4g protein; 2.9g fibre

béarnaise

2 tablespoons white vinegar
2 tablespoons water
1 shallot (25g), chopped finely
2 teaspoons coarsely chopped fresh tarragon
½ teaspoon black peppercorns
3 egg yolks
200g (6½ ounces) unsalted butter, melted
1 tablespoon finely chopped fresh tarragon

1 Combine vinegar, the water, shallot, coarsely chopped tarragon and peppercorns in small saucepan; bring to the boil then reduce heat. Simmer, uncovered, about 2 minutes or until liquid reduces by half. Strain over medium heatproof bowl; discard solids. Cool 10 minutes.
2 Whisk egg yolks into vinegar mixture until combined. Set bowl over medium saucepan of simmering water; do not let water touch base of bowl. Whisk mixture over heat until thickened.
3 Remove bowl from heat; gradually whisk in melted butter in a thin, steady stream until sauce thickens slightly. Stir in finely chopped tarragon.

prep + cook time 25 minutes **makes** 1 cup
nutritional count per tablespoon 15.1g total fat (9.5g saturated fat); 577kJ (138 cal); 0.2g carbohydrate; 0.8g protein; 0g fibre
note Serve with grilled meat, chicken or fish fillets.

white wine sauce

20g (¾ ounce) butter
2 shallots (50g), chopped finely
1 teaspoon mustard powder
¾ cup (180ml) dry white wine
¾ cup (180ml) fish stock
1¼ cups (310ml) pouring cream (see notes)

1 Melt butter in medium frying pan; cook shallot and mustard powder, stirring, about 3 minutes or until shallot softens. Add wine; cook, uncovered, until wine reduces by two-thirds. Add stock; bring to the boil. Boil, uncovered, about 7 minutes or until liquid is reduced by half.
2 Add cream to pan; bring to the boil then reduce heat. Simmer, uncovered, about 15 minutes or until sauce thickens slightly.

prep + cook time 25 minutes **makes** 1 cup
nutritional count per tablespoon 12.4g total fat (8.1g saturated fat); 531kJ (127 cal); 1g carbohydrate; 0.9g protein, 0g fibre
notes It is fine to use 1 x 300ml carton of cream for this recipe.
This is a great sauce to serve with seafood; try it with grilled or barbecued prawns or lobster or pan-fried fish fillets.

mornay

1 cup (250ml) béchamel sauce (see page 104)
¼ cup (60ml) cream
1 egg yolk
1 cup (120g) coarsely grated emmentaler cheese

1 Bring béchamel to the boil in medium saucepan; add cream and egg yolk, whisk 1 minute.
2 Remove sauce from heat; add cheese, stir until cheese melts.

prep + cook time 10 minutes **makes** 2 cups
nutritional count per tablespoon 4.4g total fat (2.8g saturated fat); 222kJ (53 cal); 1.4g carbohydrate; 2.2g protein; 0g fibre
notes Substitute gruyère or cheddar for emmentaler. Goes well with cauliflower or broccoli au gratin, lasagne and oysters.

tartare sauce

2 egg yolks
½ teaspoon salt
¾ teaspoon mustard powder
⅔ cup (160ml) extra light olive oil
⅓ cup (80ml) olive oil
1 tablespoon white vinegar
2 tablespoons finely chopped cornichons
1 tablespoon rinsed, drained baby capers, chopped finely
1 tablespoon finely chopped fresh flat-leaf parsley
2 teaspoons finely chopped fresh dill
2 teaspoons lemon juice

1 Combine egg yolks, salt and mustard in medium bowl. Gradually add combined oils, in a thin, steady stream, whisking constantly until mixture thickens.
2 Stir vinegar into mixture, then stir in remaining ingredients.

prep time 20 minutes **makes** 1 cup
nutritional count per tablespoon 19.2g total fat (2.9g saturated fat); 719kJ (172 cal); 0g carbohydrate; 0.6g protein; 0g fibre

tangy barbecue sauce

1 cup (250ml) tomato sauce (ketchup)
½ cup (125ml) cider vinegar
¼ cup (60ml) worcestershire sauce
⅔ cup (150g) firmly packed light brown sugar
2 tablespoons american-style mustard
1 fresh small red thai (serrano) chilli, chopped finely
1 clove garlic, crushed
1 tablespoon lemon juice

1 Combine ingredients in medium saucepan; bring to the boil then reduce heat. Simmer, uncovered, stirring occasionally, 20 minutes.

prep + cook time 30 minutes **makes** 2 cups
nutritional count per tablespoon 0.1g total fat (0g saturated fat); 163kJ (39 cal); 9.3g carbohydrate; 0.3g protein; 0.3g fibre

glossary

ALLSPICE also known as pimento or jamaican pepper; available whole or ground. Tastes like a blend of clove, cinnamon and nutmeg – all spices.

BASIL an aromatic herb; there are many types, but the most commonly used is sweet, or common, basil.
purple also known as opal basil; has large purple leaves and a sweet, almost gingery flavour. It has better keeping properties than most other basils. If unavailable, use sweet basil
thai also known as horapa; has smallish leaves and a sweet licorice/ aniseed taste. Available from Asian food stores and some supermarkets.

BEANS
borlotti also known as roman beans or pink beans. Interchangeable with pinto beans as they are both pale pink or beige with dark red streaks.
cannellini small white bean similar in appearance and flavour to other white beans (great northern, navy or haricot), all of which can be substituted for each other.
kidney medium-sized red bean, slightly floury in texture yet sweet in flavour.
snake long (about 40cm), thin, round, fresh green beans; Asian in origin, with a taste similar to green or french beans. They are also known as yard-long beans because of their (pre-metric) length.
sprouts also known as bean shoots; tender new growths of beans and seeds germinated for consumption.
white a generic term we use for canned or dried cannellini, haricot, navy or great northern beans.

BEEF
chuck from the neck and shoulder of the beef; tends to be chewy but flavourful and inexpensive. A good cut for stewing or braising.
gravy also known as beef shin or shank; cut from the lower shin of a cow.
corned silverside (corned beef) also known as topside roast; sold vacuum-sealed in brine.
scotch fillet also known as cube roll; cuts include rib roast and rib-eye.
sirloin cut from the lower portion of the ribs, continuing off the tenderloin.
skirt steak lean, flavourful coarsely grained cut from the inner thigh. Needs slow-cooking; good for casseroles.

BREAD
ciabatta in Italian, the word means slipper, which is the traditional shape of this popular white bread with a crisp crust.
english muffin a round teacake made from yeast, flour, milk, semolina and salt; often confused with crumpets. Pre-baked and sold packaged in supermarkets, muffins should be split open and toasted before eating.
french stick bread that's been formed into a long, narrow cylindrical loaf. It usually has a crisp brown crust and a light chewy interior. A standard stick is 5-6cm wide and 3-4cm tall, but can be up to a metre in length. It is also known as french bread, french loaf or baguette.
sourdough has a lightly sour taste from the yeast starter culture used to make the bread. A low-risen bread with a dense centre and crisp crust.

BREADCRUMBS
packaged fine-textured, crunchy, purchased white breadcrumbs.
stale one- or two-day-old bread blended or processed into crumbs.

BROCCOLINI a cross between broccoli and chinese kale; milder and sweeter than broccoli. Each long stem is topped by a loose floret that closely resembles broccoli; from floret to stem, broccolini is completely edible.

BUK CHOY also known as bok choy, pak choi, chinese white cabbage or chinese chard; has a fresh, mild mustard taste. Use both stems and leaves. Baby buk choy, also known as pak kat farang or shanghai bok choy, is smaller and more tender than buk choy.

BURGHUL also known as bulghur or bulgar wheat; hulled steamed wheat kernels that, once dried, are crushed into various size grains. Not the same as cracked wheat.

BUTTER use salted or unsalted (sweet) butter; 125g is equal to one stick of butter (4 ounces).

CAPERS the grey-green buds of a warm climate shrub (usually Mediterranean); sold either dried and salted or pickled in a vinegar brine. Baby capers are very small and have a fuller-flavour. Capers must be rinsed well before using.

CHEESE
bocconcini from the diminutive of 'boccone' meaning mouthful; a delicate, semi-soft, white cheese traditionally made from buffalo milk. Spoils rapidly, so must be kept under refrigeration, in brine, for one or two days at most.
cheddar the most widely eaten cheese in the world; a semi-hard cows'-milk cheese. It ranges in colour from white to pale yellow, and has a slightly crumbly texture if properly matured. Can be aged for up to two years, and the flavour becomes sharper with time.
emmentaler Switzerland's oldest cheese; light gold in colour with a distinctive nutty-sweet, mellow flavour. It has marble-size holes and a natural light brown rind.
fetta a crumbly goat- or sheep-milk cheese with a sharp salty taste.
gruyère a Swiss cheese having small holes and a nutty, slightly salty, flavour.
mozzarella a soft, spun-curd cheese. It has a low melting point and a wonderfully elastic texture when heated, and is used to add texture rather than flavour.
parmesan (parmigiano) a hard, grainy cows'-milk cheese.
pecorino the generic Italian name for cheeses made from sheep milk. It's a hard, white to pale yellow cheese; if unavailable, use parmesan.
ricotta the name for this soft, white, cows'-milk cheese roughly translates as 'cooked again'. It's made from whey, a by-product of other cheese-making, to which fresh milk and acid are added. Sweet and moist with a slightly grainy texture.

romano a hard sheep- or cow's-milk cheese with excellent keeping qualities. Straw-coloured and grainy in texture, it's mainly used for grating. If you can't find it, parmesan can be substituted.

CHILLI available in many types and sizes; generally the smaller the chilli, the hotter it is. Use rubber gloves when seeding and chopping fresh chillies as they can burn your skin. Removing seeds and membranes lessens the heat level.
cayenne pepper long, thin-fleshed, extremely hot red chilli usually sold dried and ground.
flakes, dried deep-red, dehydrated chilli slices and whole seeds.
green unripened chillies.
jalapeño fairly hot, green chilli, available bottled in brine, or fresh from specialty greengrocers.
long red available both fresh and dried; a generic term used for any moderately hot, long (6cm-8cm), thin chilli.
powder made from ground chillies; it can be used as a substitute for fresh chillies in the proportion of ½ teaspoon ground chilli powder to 1 chopped fresh medium chilli.
red thai a small, hot, red chilli.

CHINESE COOKING WINE also known as shao hsing or chinese rice wine; made from fermented rice, wheat, sugar and salt. Found in Asian food shops; if you can't find it, replace with mirin or sherry.

CHOY SUM also known as pakaukeo or flowering cabbage, a member of the bok choy family; easy to identify with its long stems, light green leaves and yellow flowers. Is eaten, stems and all.

CORIANDER also known as pak chee, cilantro or chinese parsley; bright-green leafy herb with a pungent flavour. Both the stems and roots of coriander are used in cooking; wash well. Also available ground or as seeds; these should not be substituted for fresh coriander as the tastes are completely different.

CORNICHONS French for gherkin, a very small variety of cucumber.

CREAM we use fresh cream, also known as pure cream and pouring cream, unless otherwise stated.

CUMIN also known as zeera or comino; has a spicy, nutty flavour.

CURRY
curry powder a blend of ground spices used for convenience when making Indian food. Choose mild or hot to suit your taste and the recipe.
green paste the hottest of the traditional pastes; contains chilli, garlic, onion, salt, lemon grass, spices and galangal.
panang paste based on the curries of Penang, an island off the north-west coast of Malaysia, close to the Thai border. A complex, sweet and milder variation of red curry paste.
red paste a very popular curry paste; a hot blend of different flavours that complements the richness of pork, duck and seafood, and also works well in marinades and sauces.
tandoori paste a highly-seasoned classic East Indian marinade flavoured with garlic, tamarind, ginger, chilli, coriander and other spices; used to give foods the authentic red-orange tint of tandoor-oven cooking.
tikka paste a medium-mild paste. In Indian cooking, this loosely translates as a non-specific paste for bite-sized pieces of meat, poultry or fish; it can be any maker's choice of spices and oils, and is frequently coloured red. Used to marinate or to brush over cooking food.

FISH FILLETS, FIRM WHITE blue eye, bream, flathead, swordfish, ling, sea perch, whiting, jewfish or snapper are all good choices. Remove any bones with tweezers.

FLOUR
plain an all-purpose wheat flour.
self-raising plain flour sifted with baking powder in the ratio of 1 cup flour to 2 teaspoons baking powder.
semolina made from durum wheat milled into various textured granules, some as fine as flour.

FRIED SHALLOTS sprinkled over just-cooked food to provide an extra crunchy finish. Purchase at all Asian grocery stores; once opened, they will keep for months if stored in a tightly sealed glass jar. Make your own by frying thinly sliced peeled shallots until golden brown and crisp.

GALANGAL a rhizome with a hot ginger-citrusy flavour; used similarly to ginger and garlic as a seasoning or an ingredient. Substitute with fresh ginger if unavailable.

GARAM MASALA a blend of cloves, cardamom, cinnamon, coriander, fennel and cumin, roasted and ground together.

GHEE clarified butter, extensively used in Indian cooking. It can be heated to higher temperatures than regular butter without burning. Available from some supermarkets.

KECAP MANIS see sauces, soy.

KITCHEN STRING made of a natural product such as cotton or hemp so that it neither affects the flavour of the food it's tied around nor melts when heated.

MARINARA MIX a mix of uncooked, chopped seafood available from fish markets, fishmongers and many larger supermarkets.

MINCE also known as ground meat.

MUSHROOMS
button small, cultivated white mushrooms with a mild flavour.
swiss browns also known as cremini or roman mushrooms; are light brown mushrooms with a full-bodied flavour. Button or cup mushrooms can be substituted.

MUSTARD
american-style bright-yellow in colour; a sweet mustard containing mustard seeds, sugar, salt, spices and garlic. Serve with hot dogs and hamburgers.
dijon a pale brown, creamy, distinctively flavoured, fairly mild French-style mustard.
powder finely ground white (yellow) mustard seeds.

wholegrain also known as seeded. A French-style coarse-grain mustard made from crushed mustard seeds and dijon-style french mustard.

NOODLES, SINGAPORE these pre-cooked wheat noodles are best described as a thinner version of hokkien; sold, packaged, in the refrigerated section of supermarkets.

PANCETTA cured (not smoked) pork belly; bacon can be substituted.

PAPRIKA ground, dried, sweet red capsicum (bell pepper); there are many types available, including sweet, hot, mild and smoked.

PATTY-PAN SQUASH also known as crookneck or custard marrow pumpkins; a round, slightly flat summer squash being yellow to pale-green in colour and having a scalloped edge. It has a firm white flesh and a distinct flavour.

PEARL BARLEY barley that has had its outer husk (bran) removed, and been steamed and polished, much the same as rice.

POLENTA also known as cornmeal; a flour-like cereal made of ground corn (maize). Also the name of the dish made from it.

RICE
arborio small, round-grained rice; absorbs a large amount of liquid.
jasmine fragrant long-grained rice; white rice can be substituted, but will not taste the same.
wild rice blend a mixture of white long-grain and dark brown wild rice. The latter is the seed of a North American aquatic grass, which has a distinctively nutty flavour and a crunchy, resilient texture.

SAKE Japan's favourite wine, made from fermented rice. If unavailable, dry sherry, vermouth or brandy can be substituted. Cooking sake (containing salt) is also available.

SAMBAL OELEK (also ulek or olek) Indonesian in origin; a salty paste made from ground chillies and vinegar. Found in supermarkets and Asian food stores.

SAUCES
black bean a Chinese sauce made from fermented soya beans, spices, water and wheat flour.
char siu a Chinese barbecue sauce made from sugar, water, salt, honey, fermented soya bean paste, soy sauce, malt syrup and spices. It can be found at most supermarkets.
chilli we use a hot Chinese variety made from red thai chillies, salt and vinegar. Use sparingly, increasing the quantity to suit your taste.
fish also called nam pla or nuoc nam; made from pulverised salted fermented fish, most often anchovies. Has a pungent smell and strong taste, so use sparingly.
hoisin a thick, sweet and spicy Chinese sauce made from salted soya beans, onions and garlic.
oyster a rich, brown sauce made from oysters and their brine and cooked with salt and soy sauce, and thickened with starches.
soy also known as sieu; made from fermented soya beans. Several variations are available in most supermarkets and Asian food stores. We use a mild Japanese variety in our recipes; possibly the best table soy and the one to choose if you only want one variety.
dark soy deep brown, almost black in colour; rich, with a thicker consistency than other types. Pungent, but not particularly salty.
kecap manis a dark, thick, sweet soy sauce. Depending on the brand, the soy's sweetness is derived from the addition of either molasses or palm sugar when brewed.
light soy fairly thin in consistency and, while paler than the others, the saltiest tasting; used in dishes in which the natural colour of the ingredients is to be maintained. Don't confuse with salt-reduced or low-sodium soy sauces.
sweet chilli a fairly mild, Thai-style sauce made from red chillies, sugar, garlic and vinegar.
tomato pasta made from a blend of tomatoes, herbs and spices.
vegetarian mushroom oyster made from mushrooms and soy sauce.
worcestershire a dark-coloured sauce made from garlic, soy sauce, tamarind, onions, molasses, lime, anchovies, vinegar and seasonings.

SUGAR
brown very soft, finely granulated sugar retaining molasses for its characteristic colour and flavour. Dark brown sugar may be used.
caster also known as superfine or finely granulated table sugar.
raw brown coarse-grained sugar.
white a coarsely granulated table sugar, also known as crystal sugar.

TACO SEASONING MIX meant to duplicate the taste of a Mexican sauce made from oregano, cumin, chillies and other spices.

TAMARIND CONCENTRATE the commercial distillation of tamarind pulp into a condensed paste. Used straight from the container, with no soaking or straining required, although it can be diluted with water according to taste. Found in supermarkets and Asian food stores. It adds a tart, sour taste to food.

VINEGAR
balsamic made from the juice of Trebbiano grapes; it is a deep rich brown colour with a sweet and sour flavour. Quality can be determined up to a point by price; use the most expensive sparingly.
brown malt made from fermented malt and beech shavings.
raspberry fresh raspberries steeped in a white wine vinegar.
red wine based on red wine.
rice a colourless vinegar made from fermented rice, sugar and salt. Also known as seasoned rice vinegar.
sherry made from a blend of wines left in wood vats to mature where they develop a rich mellow flavour.
white made from spirit of cane sugar.
white wine made from white wine.

WATERCRESS a large group of peppery greens. Highly perishable, so must be used as soon as possible after purchase.

conversion chart

MEASURES

One Australian metric measuring cup holds approximately 250ml; one Australian metric tablespoon holds 20ml; one Australian metric teaspoon holds 5ml.

The difference between one country's measuring cups and another's is within a two- or three-teaspoon variance, and will not affect your cooking results. North America, New Zealand and the United Kingdom use a 15ml tablespoon.

All cup and spoon measurements are level. The most accurate way of measuring dry ingredients is to weigh them. When measuring liquids, use a clear glass or plastic jug with the metric markings.

We use large eggs with an average weight of 60g.

DRY MEASURES

METRIC	IMPERIAL
15g	½oz
30g	1oz
60g	2oz
90g	3oz
125g	4oz (¼lb)
155g	5oz
185g	6oz
220g	7oz
250g	8oz (½lb)
280g	9oz
315g	10oz
345g	11oz
375g	12oz (¾lb)
410g	13oz
440g	14oz
470g	15oz
500g	16oz (1lb)
750g	24oz (1½lb)
1kg	32oz (2lb)

LIQUID MEASURES

METRIC	IMPERIAL
30ml	1 fluid oz
60ml	2 fluid oz
100ml	3 fluid oz
125ml	4 fluid oz
150ml	5 fluid oz
190ml	6 fluid oz
250ml	8 fluid oz
300ml	10 fluid oz
500ml	16 fluid oz
600ml	20 fluid oz
1000ml (1 litre)	1¾ pints

LENGTH MEASURES

METRIC	IMPERIAL
3mm	⅛in
6mm	¼in
1cm	½in
2cm	¾in
2.5cm	1in
5cm	2in
6cm	2½in
8cm	3in
10cm	4in
13cm	5in
15cm	6in
18cm	7in
20cm	8in
23cm	9in
25cm	10in
28cm	11in
30cm	12in (1ft)

OVEN TEMPERATURES

The oven temperatures in this book are for conventional ovens; if you have a fan-forced oven, decrease the temperature by 10-20 degrees.

	°C (CELSIUS)	°F (FAHRENHEIT)
Very slow	120	250
Slow	150	300
Moderately slow	160	325
Moderate	180	350
Moderately hot	200	400
Hot	220	425
Very hot	240	475

index

Published in 2010 by ACP Books, Sydney
ACP Books are published by ACP Magazines
a division of PBL Media Pty Limited

ACP BOOKS

General manager Christine Whiston
Editor-in-chief Susan Tomnay
Creative director & designer Hieu Chi Nguyen
Art director Hannah Blackmore
Design assistant Sarah Holmes
Senior editor Wendy Bryant
Food director Pamela Clark
Food editor Cathie Lonnie
Nutritional information Jordanna Levin
Sales & rights director Brian Cearnes
Marketing manager Bridget Cody
Senior business analyst Rebecca Varela
Circulation manager Jama Mclean
Operations manager David Scotto
Production manager Victoria Jefferys

Published by ACP Books, a division of ACP Magazines Ltd, 54 Park St, Sydney;
GPO Box 4088, Sydney, NSW 2001.
Phone (02) 9282 8618; fax (02) 9267 9438.

acpbooks@acpmagazines.com.au;
www.acpbooks.com.au

Printed by Toppan Printing Co, China.

United Kingdom Distributed by Australian Consolidated Press (UK),
Phone (01604) 642 200; fax (01604) 642 300; books@acpuk.com

Title: Back to basics / food director Pamela Clark.
ISBN: 978 186396 939 0 (pbk.)
Notes: Includes index.
Subjects: Quick and easy cookery.
Other Authors/Contributors: Clark, Pamela.
Dewey Number: 641.512

ABN 18 053 273 546

Cover Spaghetti and meatballs, page 64
Photographer Tanya Zouev
Stylist Vicki Liley
Food preparation Ariarne Bradshaw

Send recipe enquiries to: recipeenquiries@acpmagazines.com.au